"Thank you, Sissy, for writing such a t[ ] about girls and anxiety. No one we knov. on this issue than Sissy Goff. She has done more for girls and young women than anyone we have ever known, and this important book couldn't have come at a better time. As parents of a beautiful daughter, we are so grateful."

—Tracie Hamilton, wife, mother, humanitarian,
and Haiti activist

—Scott Hamilton, husband, father, cancer activist,
and Olympic gold medalist

"Scripture tells us 'in this world you will have trouble' (John 16:33). I'm thankful that God has Sissy Goff in this world to come alongside girls and young women where they are as worriers and grow them gracefully with grit into *warriors*—encouraged and strengthened in spirit for all that will come their way."

—Elisabeth Hasselbeck, daughter of a King; wife to Tim;
mom to Grace, Taylor, and Isaiah; author of *Point of View*

"The moment I heard my go-to girl expert, Sissy Goff, was writing a book on fear/worry/anxiety, I couldn't wait for it to be published. Countless moms reach out to me, desperate for resources to help their girls become worry-free. In these pages you will find comfort in knowing not only the reasons why your daughter struggles but also how you can help her. Sissy offers hope you can both move toward. She has hands-on, daily experience counseling families through anxiety, and now that expertise and wisdom is available to you. Even though I'm a mom to four boys, I believe Sissy's work will embolden a generation of girls to stop underestimating themselves and overestimating threats."

—Heather MacFadyen, host of the *Don't Mom Alone* podcast

"This is one of those parenting books that catches you off guard in the best possible way. As a dad of daughters, I read it thinking

I would learn a lot about my kids, but I ended up finding out a lot about myself too. This guide will do wonders for families."

—Jon Acuff, *New York Times* bestselling author
of *Finish: Give Yourself the Gift of Done*

"I can't think of a single counselor more qualified to write a book on raising worry-free girls than Sissy Goff. *Raising Worry-Free Girls* is practical, biblical, and extraordinarily helpful. If you read only one book on helping your daughter understand, navigate, and overcome her anxiety, make it this one."

—Jeannie Cunnion, author of *Mom Set Free*

"I met Sissy weeks after my wife, Wynter, suddenly died. But when I met her it was if I had known her my entire life. Sissy has the unique ability to guide you and your girl in truth and love, and point you toward the Light."

—Jonathan Pitts, president of For Girls Like You Ministries

"Sissy Goff is a gem. Her deep wisdom, compassion, and knowledge helps parents of girls navigate the uncertain waters of modern childhood and adolescence. This anxiety epidemic is an urgent issue to address—both in our daughters lives, as well as our own."

—Shannon Millard, wife of Bart Millard, lead singer of MercyMe

"Girls all around our communities are losing much more than sleep over worry and anxiety. They are losing hope, joy, faith, and even the will to live. I wholeheartedly believe this is the book that could change the course of the anxiety epidemic. Parents, let's commit to crushing the Worry Monster for the next generation!"

—Courtney DeFeo, author of *In This House, We Will Giggle* and
the *Treasured* study (for tween girls and moms)

RAISING WORRY-FREE GIRLS

HELPING YOUR DAUGHTER FEEL BRAVER, STRONGER, and SMARTER in an ANXIOUS WORLD

Sissy Goff, *MEd, LPC-MHSP*

BETHANYHOUSE

a division of Baker Publishing Group
Minneapolis, Minnesota

Published by Bethany House Publishers
11400 Hampshire Avenue South
Bloomington, Minnesota 55438
www.bethanyhouse.com

Bethany House Publishers is a division of
Baker Publishing Group, Grand Rapids, Michigan

Printed in the United States of America

Library of Congress Cataloging-in-Publication Data
Names: Goff, Sissy, author.
Title: Raising worry-free girls : helping your daughter feel braver, stronger, and smarter in
    an anxious world / Sissy Goff MEd, LPC-MHSP.
Description: Bloomington, Minnesota : Bethany House Publishers, [2019] | Includes
    bibliographical references.
Identifiers: LCCN 2019019806| ISBN 9780764233401 (trade paper : alk. paper) | ISBN
    9781493421862 (ebook)
Subjects: LCSH: Parenting—Religious aspects—Christianity. | Daughters. | Anxiety. |
    Anxiety—Religious aspects—Christianity.
Classification: LCC BV4529 .G636 2019 | DDC 649/.133—dc23
LC record available at https://lccn.loc.gov/2019019806

Some names and recognizable details have been changed to protect the privacy of those who have shared their stories for this book.

Cover design by Connie Gabbert.

Baker Publishing Group publications use paper produced from sustainable forestry practices and post-consumer waste whenever possible.

24 25 26 27   12 11 10 9

For my mom.

Thank you for being the brave, strong, smart woman
you truly are and have inspired me to be.

Contents

Foreword

Growing up, I was a worrier. I worried that my parents would die. I worried that my dog would get hit by a car. I worried that I worried too much. I was that kid. But I muscled my way through it. And then as an adult, by the grace of God, I found an incredible therapist who helped me finally get past my worry. And now I travel the world, writing books and speaking on stages, helping other people overcome their worries.

So you can imagine my fear when I walked into my daughter's bedroom a few years back and found her crying because she was worried that I would die. The thing was, I wasn't sick. I was perfectly healthy. In the months that followed, my child's worry grew, and we knew we needed help. Enter Sissy Goff.

After two appointments with Sissy, my kid was a completely different human being. What in the world had happened?

I'll tell you exactly what my daughter told me: "I realized I'm more brave than I am afraid. So even though I'm afraid sometimes, I'm brave most of the time."

That's it. Identifying that singular truth propelled her worry into the abyss and began her healing. And now, five years later, I marvel at the strength and bravery of my former worrier.

This book is a gold mine—a true gold mine of tools that will help us begin to wage war against this epidemic of worry that is sweeping the world. But not just tools for your girl. Tools for YOU. So read it, and begin to feel the breath of hope fill your lungs like you haven't felt in a very long time.

Your kid's worry is about to be defeated.

—Carlos Whittaker, author of *Kill the Spider*

Introduction

You've found your way to this book, which means you're likely worried about a child you love. Maybe your third-grade daughter is a constant worrier. She asks what-if question after what-if question. Maybe you've heard talk among your friends about anxiety and felt like it possibly describes your middle schooler. Maybe you've read about the looping thoughts that often characterize anxiety and have noticed that your granddaughter gets stuck on certain thoughts regularly. Maybe transitions are hard for one of your kids. Maybe your daughter gets angry often, and there seems to be more to it than typical teenage stubbornness. Maybe you just really want your daughter to discover the bravery and strength you know God has placed inside of her.

Whatever the situation is, I'm glad you picked up this book.

I'm glad for several reasons. For starters, we are clearly living in an anxious world. Worry has woven its way through the generations and has profoundly impacted the lives of the kids we love. In fact, anxiety is a childhood epidemic in America today. I've been counseling children and teenagers for more than twenty-five years, and I've never seen anything sweep the lives of kids like worry and anxiety have in the last few years. When I first started counseling, probably one out of every twenty kids coming in was dealing with anxiety. Now, at least sixteen of every twenty new appointments are for that reason. It truly is an epidemic.

And because anxiety is an epidemic among children, it's also an epidemic among parents. Yes, anxiety does have a genetic component, which we'll discuss in a later chapter. We'll also learn about the worry continuum and how all of us fall somewhere along it. But I sit with parents every day who are consumed with worry because their daughter is consumed with worry.

I would guess you feel something along those lines too. You don't know how to help. You feel lost. And it seems like the things you do often make matters worse.

I truly believe the advice and insights in this book can make a difference. Along the way, you'll find tips and tricks to help your daughter work through her worries and find her voice, to help her fight anxiety so that it no longer has power over her. But here's a warning: Good counseling makes you uncomfortable, and this book most likely will too. The primary focus will be on your child, but we're going to talk about you too.

If you were to bring your child to my office for counseling, I'd spend time with her, as well as you. I'd want you to learn the tools she finds that help so that you can remind and prompt her when worried thoughts come. But we'd also talk some about you—if there's a history of anxiety in your family, if you've struggled with it yourself. Research shows that one of the biggest predictors of anxiety in kids is anxiety in parents. It perpetuates for several reasons, one of which is that *our* fear sometimes gets in the way of them doing what they need to do to work through *their* fear.

Our goal is for the child you love to know that she is smart, capable, brave, strong, and resilient. We want her to grow in her grit.

Growth often involves struggle. It can hurt to see your child face challenges, so her growing pains may feel more painful to you than to her. What I've experienced in my office is that it is sometimes the best-intentioned, most loving, most caring parents who have the hardest time in the struggle. The journey is hers. But it's yours too. I promise you'll all come out stronger for it. And braver.

Because the journey is one that you will both take, the main sections and chapters of this book mirror those in a companion activity book for elementary-aged girls called *Braver, Stronger, Smarter*. This book and hers start by establishing a foundational **understanding** of anxiety and how all of us deal with it to some degree. We want to be aware of the differences between fear, worry, and anxiety and of what might be impacting the girl you love. Then we'll talk about **help**. It's what parents ask for the most in my office.

"What can I do to help?"

"Can you give her tools to work through the anxiety?"

"What are some coping strategies that she can use now but also down the road, if things get tough again?"

Although anxiety is the most common disorder in childhood, it's also the most treatable, according to Dr. Tamar Chansky of worrywisekids.org.[1] So there is a lot of good news. We'll talk about a variety of skills she can use for the rest of her life when anxiety-provoking situations come up. And finally, we'll move to what I consider the most important section of each book: **hope**. There is great research and material about using cognitive, emotional, and practical perspectives to combat anxiety. But there is not much available that talks about how to work through worry from the place I believe makes the most profound difference: our faith in God. In that final section on hope, we'll look at John 16:33:

> "I have told you these things, so that in me you may have peace. In this world you will have trouble. But take heart! I have overcome the world."

In this world, you and I will indeed have trouble. Our girls will face it too. But in the midst of those troubles, we can take heart because God has overcome the world. We want our girls to have a faith in God that not only informs their decisions but informs their hearts. We want their spiritual lives to be the ballast that anchors them when emotions toss them about. As a counselor, however, I would say that is happening to a lesser and lesser degree among kids than ever before.

Which reminds me, I haven't really introduced myself properly yet. I mentioned that I've been counseling kids and their families for over twenty-five years. Along with my dear friends Melissa Trevathan and David Thomas, I've also written a handful of parenting books and have the privilege of speaking to parents all over the country under the banner of Raising Boys and Girls. Our website is anchored with the words: "Parenting is a challenging, delightful, heart-wrenching journey that can feel profoundly overwhelming and lonely at times. Parents need guides who understand the world of their children."[2]

Parenting a child who struggles with anxiety is particularly challenging and heart-wrenching. But it can also be delightful and empowering and hopeful—for the child you love *and* for you. I'm honored to be a part of your journey. And I'm looking forward to us growing together.

UNDERSTANDING

1. Defining Worry

What I am about to say may sound a little crazy.

But think back to times when you have driven over a bridge. Perhaps you were in the car by yourself. Maybe having a bit of a stressful day . . . but maybe not. As you drive across, though, a flash of a thought hits. *If I turned my wheel just a little bit to the right, I could crash over the edge.*

Please tell me I'm not the only one who has thoughts like this come out of the blue. For you, they may involve imagining a plane crash or some other scary situation. It doesn't mean we're crazy or suicidal. It's usually just a moment that passes, and we go on with our day, never giving it another thought.

Here's the thing. We all have random flashes of troubling thoughts sometimes. In fact, the average person has dozens, maybe even hundreds, of what we call *intrusive thoughts* per day.[1] As an adult, I know I can say them out loud, hoping—assuming—that you've had them too. And so I don't really feel crazy. Or alone.

Kids, however, are different. Especially girls, I believe.

By nature, girls want to please. Girls define themselves against a backdrop of relationship. Feeling known and loved is crucial. So to say something that might sound crazy or weird, or might make others reject them, can feel like a terrible risk. *You might not like me anymore,* they think. *Even more than that, you might not love me. You might think I'm crazy. Maybe I am. . . .*

And so the thought that should be a flash gets stuck. It becomes what I refer to daily in my offices as the one-loop roller coaster at the fair. The thought goes around and around and around in the quiet of kids' heads and becomes deafening.

I feel sick. I'm going to throw up.

I can't go to school. No one there likes me.

I have to check and recheck this until I get it right. I can't mess up.

A little fear becomes a big worry. And that worry loops around and around and around . . . until it feels a lot like a gigantic, catastrophic, insurmountable monster of anxiety. We'll call him the Worry Monster.

In her worries, your daughter often feels alone. She doesn't know that others feel the same way, because it's too scary to put her worries into words. Maybe people won't like her. Or they'll think she's weird. So she thinks she's the only one and that something *is* wrong with her.

This isn't unusual. When something goes wrong in a girl's world, she usually blames herself. (Boys are much more likely to blame someone else, such as Mom. Sorry, moms.) She doesn't yet know about the Worry Monster. We're going to talk a lot about him in the pages ahead, and even more in the pages of the book for her: *Braver, Stronger, Smarter*.

It doesn't help that we adults often don't know she's battling a worry monster. We only see her tears. Or anger. Or hear the endless questions. Her outsides don't match her insides, and her worries come out sideways through a whole host of other emotions. We don't understand. Neither does she.

The more she listens to the tricks the Worry Monster tries to play on her, the stronger he gets. But the more we learn about her Worry Monster, the weaker he gets. So, let's start with learning about the worry continuum.

The Worry Continuum

Starting with Fear

Quick—name one thing you're afraid of. Now, one thing your daughter is afraid of.

When we use the word *afraid*, "of" often comes after it. *Of* means there's something following it. Or a couple of somethings. It's tied to the specific: spiders, monsters, speaking in public, etc. We all have fears of one kind or another. Some of us have more fears than others. Children share similar fears at certain ages. In fact, there are normal childhood fears that occur throughout their development.

Infants' and toddlers' normal fears revolve around separation— usually separation from you. They're also afraid of strangers, loud noises, and sudden movements.

Preschool-aged children are in a stage of learning what's real and what's not. Many of their fears center around those types of things: the dark, monsters, ghosts, and then things that many of us wish weren't real, like snakes, spiders, and doctors' shots.

Elementary-school-aged children are entering an age of awareness. They're suddenly old enough to know a little of what's going on in the news and the world around them, so their fears center more on real-life dangers. They tend to be fearful of events such as losing a loved one, being kidnapped, storms, and death.

Middle-school-aged children are much more focused on (we could even say consumed by) the world of their peers. So their fears are related to being accepted by or ashamed in front of those peers. Their fears can also be connected to where they're placing their burgeoning identities. If your daughter is inclined toward academics, she might be afraid of failing a test. If it's athletics, her fear might be missing a shot or performing poorly in a track meet. If she's into acting, she might be afraid of forgetting her lines. Almost every middle schooler is afraid of giving a speech in front of their class.

High-school-aged kids' fears often involve the same types of things their middle school fears did. But the stakes are higher now—and more intimate. They're afraid of rejection by either friends or a love interest. They're afraid of not having friends or a love interest. They're afraid of the future and their readiness for it. They're feeling pressure about future-oriented choices, including "fun" things like standardized tests, college, and what they're going to do with the rest of their lives.

With typical developmental fears, the operative word is *developmental*. Kids usually grow out of these fears. Toddlers have enough experiences with babysitters who order pizza and bring their own crafts that they realize it's actually kind of fun to have a babysitter. Young children learn that monsters don't really live under their beds. Your elementary-aged daughter goes upstairs alone enough times to finally feel comfortable doing it without you waiting at the bottom of the stairs. Toddlers become preschoolers, who become middle schoolers, who become high schoolers, who become adults mostly unscathed by their passing fears.

Fear passage involves two primary factors: experience and trust. As a kid, you experienced that the thing you were most afraid of didn't happen. You gave the speech, your face turned red, maybe your tummy even got upset, but you lived through it. You still had friends. You even got a pretty good grade. It wasn't so much that you experienced success. You experienced survival. You made it through. And when you make it through enough scary times, the fear passes.

However, there are times when the thing you're afraid of does happen. The storm really did get bad and turned into a tornado. Maybe that tornado even passed down your street.

Several years ago, I met with a nine-year-old girl whose primary fear was being away from her mom. She hated to be away from her, and when they were separated, she was afraid her mom would get hurt.

Her mom brought her in to see me right before a vacation she was taking with her dad—without their daughter. The girl was terrified that her mom was going to get into a car accident and die. During our session, we talked a lot about experience, but we also talked more specifically about evidence (something we'll come back to in the next section on help).

I asked a number of questions, trying to get the girl to see how little evidence there was for her fears.

"How many miles does your mom drive each week?" (You can guess the answer: somewhere in the hundreds.)

"Has your mom ever had a car accident?"

"Maybe one or two," she replied.

"So, over the twenty years she's been driving, she's only had one or two accidents." (I have a feeling this girl didn't really know her mom's driving record, but I decided to go with it.) "Do you think that means your mom is a good driver?"

"Yes."

"Is your mom smart?"

"Yes."

"Does she try her best to keep everyone safe, including herself?"

"Yes."

"Then, do you really think your mom is going to have a car accident, based on the evidence?"

"No, I don't," she said. And a big smile spread across her face.

Now, let me tell you the rest of the story. My sessions start on the hour. But when my time with the girl ended, her mom hadn't returned. I knew she was highly responsible (which was what made me feel safe to talk about her driving record), so when she wasn't there at ten minutes, then fifteen minutes, then twenty minutes after, I was concerned. And, since this little girl was already bent toward worry, she was *really* concerned. We went to sit out on the front porch to wait on her mom.

Finally, her mom ran up from the parking lot. From the edge of the Daystar Counseling lawn, she threw her hands up and shouted, laughing, "You'll never believe why I was late. I had a wreck!"

I couldn't believe it. *Seriously?* The little girl looked at me with the widest eyes you've ever seen. I expected tears, but they never came because her smart mom was laughing. She didn't act like the car accident was a big deal at all. I took my cue from her and started laughing too. "Of all the things, we were just talking about car accidents." I turned to the girl and said, "Your mom is a good driver, and, look, she had an accident, but she's fine!"

That nine-year-old girl is now fourteen and no longer afraid of her mom getting in a car accident. In fact, she doesn't even think about her mom much at all—welcome to adolescence! Her fear passed. Her mom had a wreck that day but didn't on the ensuing trip with her dad. Or their family's next trip. Over time, the girl's experience led to trust—helped by the fact that her mom didn't catastrophize the incident, another idea that we'll come back to later. This girl and her mom also have a faith that makes a difference—more about that in the last section of the book.

For now, let's remember that **fears are a normal part of childhood.** They come and go, based on your daughter's developmental level. With experience and trust, time passes and fears pass. She comes through all the stronger for it. Unless she doesn't, and those fears of hers grow into a more lingering sense of worry.

Moving to Worry

With worry, the scope gets a little broader. We're worried "about," rather than afraid "of."

Now my questions become, What is one thing you're worried about? One thing your daughter is worried about?

We worry more about concepts than specific things. You don't necessarily worry about spiders. But you worry about bad things happening to someone you love. Fear is narrower than worry but can move into worry, with the right (or wrong) set of circumstances. Fear moves to worry based partially on our experiences.

For example, I grew up in Arkansas and now live in Tennessee, so I worry that a storm might turn into a tornado more than someone who lives near the beach in Florida does. But she might worry a little more about hurricanes. I'm not worried about a hurricane one bit here in the landlocked South. Fears turn into worry when the evidence of your experience means something bad really does have a greater likelihood of happening.

If you're a student of the Enneagram personality types, you know people with certain "numbers" are more predisposed to worry. A person who is a six, for example, is described as the Loyalist and leans toward worry. My sister (a six) describes fellow sixes like ducks. When they swim, they look unruffled on the surface, but beneath the water their little legs are paddling like crazy. Whatever it is that is causing us to paddle about, worries leave us with a wider, more lingering sense of concern than fears do. (To learn more about the Enneagram, one book I'd suggest is *The Road Back to You* by Ian Morgan Cron and Suzanne Stabile.)

Worries tend to be future oriented. For infants and toddlers, this means they don't experience worry for very long, because they live so much in the present. Your little one, upon seeing you pick up your car keys, might worry that you're leaving her at home with the babysitter. A young child walking through Disney World might worry that she'll round the corner and run into Maleficent or another Disney villain. If you fly to visit an old friend, your elementary-aged child may worry that your plane will crash. A middle schooler will likely worry about her social status and what others think about her. Every high school junior and senior I have ever counseled is worried about what happens next, even if they don't act like it with you, as their parent. And the worries go on well into adulthood. Again, ahem, maybe you worry about your kids from time to time?

All is not lost, though.

When your daughter has a little help, a lot of empowerment, and a foundational faith, worries don't have to carry the same power in her life. With God's help, I really believe you *can* raise a worry-free girl. As *The Message* paraphrase of Matthew 11:28–30 says,

"Are you tired? Worn out? Burned out on religion? Come to me. Get away with me and you'll recover your life. I'll show you how to take a real rest. Walk with me and work with me—watch how I do it. Learn the unforced rhythms of grace. I won't lay anything heavy or ill-fitting on you. Keep company with me and you'll learn to live freely and lightly."

Worries come and go. It's how you and she respond that makes the difference. Our goal is to understand fear, move through worries, and help her not get stuck in a loop of anxiety.

Children actually develop their own strategies for coping with worry. Your daughter has some right now that she probably doesn't even know are strategies. Again, we'll come back to those. We'll also learn how to give her even more tools that can help when the inevitable worries come.

Landing in Anxiety

Worry turns into anxiety for a variety of reasons. Trauma can cause a child who worries to develop anxiety. Genetics can, as well (again, we'll come back to that in the next chapter). Personality, environment, life circumstances, and a whole host of factors can cause a child who worries to become a child with anxiety. As I said, fears pass with time, experience, and trust. Worries come and go, for all of us. But anxiety, left untreated, only gets worse.

With anxiety, we've got a really wide scope. It's not "of" or "about" something. It's "I have" or "I am."

It's a state of being: "I have anxiety," "I am anxious." And sadly, this state often comes to define us or the kids we love. In all my years of counseling, I've never had so many girls give me "I am" statements about anxiety as they have in the past five or so years.

Just as there is a continuum from fear to anxiety, there is also a continuum within anxiety itself. Anxiety looks different on different girls. It varies in intensity and expression. We'll describe those girls and the differences in their anxiety in the next chapter. Clinically, there are several types of anxiety, including the most common: generalized anxiety disorder (GAD); they are described in Appendix 1. But for now, I want to use the word *anxiety* in a more general sense and define it as a state of perpetual worry—a state that either returns frequently or just never quite seems to lift.

Anxiety is perpetual worry and also constant pressure. A girl with anxiety feels pressure to be sure about things. To be in control. To get it right. To know what's coming. To do anything and everything to prevent the dreaded thing (in her anxious way of thinking) from happening.

Girls with anxiety overestimate the threat and underestimate themselves and their ability to cope. The worst-case scenario becomes a normal life perspective.

Anxieties also follow along with a child's development. If we were to talk about a toddler and anxiety, we'd be talking about separation anxiety. I've counseled many elementary-aged girls who live with anxiety around something bad happening to one of their parents. In this age when statistics show suicide is on the rise, I also see a lot of girls from elementary school age through their teenage years who have anxiety related to suicide. It's not that they're suicidal. It's more that they're afraid they might accidentally do the scariest thing they've ever heard of. (Remember the bridge thought at the beginning of the chapter?) I have seen many girls over the years feel anxious about possibly vomiting in class. As you might guess, more often than not, they're in fifth or sixth grade. They're starting middle school, and the worst thing they can imagine is embarrassing themselves in front of their friends. Plus, it's kind of miserable in every way to throw up. For high school girls, their anxiety is bound up in performance or relationships. In the culture we're living in now, it's also often tied to their sexuality.

We're all afraid of these things from time to time. However, these children don't just think about them once or from time to time. They have the same flash of a scary thought. But, remember, with anxiety they overestimate the problem and underestimate themselves. A slight chance becomes a huge risk that they can't let go of. And so the anxious thought starts to loop and goes around and around and around.

A psychiatrist with whom I work regularly and whom I respect a great deal said to me several years ago, "Kids have anxiety around whatever is basically the worst thing they can imagine happening at their age. With teenagers, those thoughts are most often violent or sexual in nature."

At the time, I was counseling a girl in high school who was having both sexual and violent thoughts toward certain people, including her friends and even the children she babysat. But, let me tell you, no one would have ever known. She was the kind of teenager you'd want your daughter to grow up to be like. She was a leader among her peers. She was kind and conscientious and tried hard in most everything she did. But she was riddled with anxiety. In fact, we talked a great deal about how those thoughts weren't her. They were her anxiety trying to take over. Remember that old Worry Monster? I don't honestly believe she was capable of or even wanted to do those things. But she had a flash of a thought, and it got stuck. And she literally thought she was going crazy. Her anxiety was rooted in an overestimation of the problem and a lack of trust in herself. It took her months to feel safe enough to say the words that were looping in her head out loud to me. And when she did, there was so much shame that came out with them.

Another primary factor of anxiety is that **anxiety is born out of fear but has a response that is disproportionate to the fear itself.** This summer at our camp, a girl cried and yelled for over an hour because she had to walk through a swarm of bugs to get to the lake. Her response was disproportionate to her fear, although I'll admit the bugs were awfully yucky.

Because anxiety shows up in children in different ways, the Worry Monster can be sneaky and hard to recognize. Some anxious children will scream and cry. They will rage at you if you disrupt their schedule or system. Or maybe they won't. Their responses may be huge and loud and feel attention seeking. Or, they may quietly spend hours going over and over and over the same math problems to get them just right.

Maybe you've noticed that your daughter seems to have more fears than her friends do. Maybe she talks often about worst-case scenarios. Maybe her teacher has mentioned anxiety. Or your girl has. Whatever the situation, I know you want your daughter to feel braver, stronger, and smarter. You want her to have a faith that brings her peace and comfort. But, right now, it's not happening. The Worry Monster seems to have a bigger voice than she does. And, because her Worry Monster is in control, your Worry Monster is starting to turn up the volume with you.

When You Need to Worry about Her Level of Worry

From my experience, I am guessing that reading all this could have you more concerned than before. You've already seen your daughter several times in these pages. If you have, I don't want you to worry. My hope is that this book is going to work me out of a job. I will teach you anxiety-fighting strategies to try at home first. Your relationship and teamwork as she fights her Worry Monster are going to be her most important weapons for beating him.

For some girls, however, an understanding of worry and the tools to battle it may not be enough. As a counselor, I often compare the therapeutic process to a cold or sinus infection. Physicians won't give you antibiotics at first, because they want your immune system to do the work, knowing that your immune system becomes stronger for having fought off the infection. There is a great chance that, between you and your daughter, she has everything she needs to fight the Worry Monster. She will still worry from time to time, but through this book (and, if she's elementary-aged, the companion activity book), she'll know his tricks and have the tools to manage her worry. She'll actually be stronger for having fought the battle. But sometimes your immune system just can't take down the infection on its own. In those times, you need an antibiotic.

The antibiotic for her anxiety may simply be taking her to therapy. Counseling may sound scary, but it doesn't have to be. We often say at Daystar that we're not telling kids anything different than you are, as their parents. We're just a new voice, so they sometimes hear us a little louder. We also have the training and experience to help kids battle anxiety. If it feels like you're not enough to help her, it's not really because you're not enough. It's that her anxiety has taken root to the degree that she just needs a stronger antibiotic.

"How do I find the right counselor?" you may be wondering. There are counselors all over the world who do fantastic work with kids. It can be a great idea to interview the counselor yourself first. Go to their office. If you have a young child, make sure the office is kid friendly. You want to find a counselor who is warm and kind but can also be strong when needed. And, obviously, you want a therapist who has good training and experience in counseling children. And those, by the way, are all appropriate things to ask about.

Every time my colleagues and I travel and speak across the country, we're approached about counselors in that particular city. I wish we had a referral base for counselors we know and trust in every city. We haven't quite gotten there, but your school or your church can be a great source for referrals. They know from experience who works well with children and adolescents. Don't be afraid to reach out. In this day and time, anyone who loves kids knows that children and parents alike need support. And that is the bottom line of what all of us who call ourselves counselors and therapists are: support for your child and for you. We're an extension of your team for however long you need us.

As a counselor, I need to say that there are times when therapy isn't enough and medication is needed. Some of the most common medications are selective serotonin reuptake inhibitors, or SSRI medications. Years ago, a psychiatrist explained SSRI medications to me. He talked about the brain like two cars. He described synapses, those gaps in the nerve cells of our brains we studied in science class as kids. He said that serotonin fires across the synapses, keeping our brains working the way they're supposed to—keeping us emotionally and mentally healthy. When we're sad or anxious for a long enough period, the serotonin stops firing. At that point, no amount of therapy or intervention strategies can help other than a replacement for the serotonin. He likened medication to a jumper cable stretching from one end of a synapse to the next. Medication gets it firing again.

I know many parents are fearful of medication because of certain studies and statistics they might have read. I understand your concern. I believe medication should be the last resort for children. Unfortunately, in our culture, many parents are more likely to medicate their children than provide them with therapy. I do believe therapy makes a profound difference. But I have had hundreds of situations in my counseling office where medication was necessary for the emotional and mental health of a child. I've also had thousands of children who haven't needed medication, for whom therapy was enough. While I do believe medicine is necessary at times, I would not move forward into the arena of medicine without pursuing therapy first and consulting with a child psychiatrist.

When should you take your daughter to therapy?

- If you've already attempted to help your daughter on your own with specific strategies designed for anxiety, such as the strategies contained in this book, and they haven't made a difference.
- If your child has suffered from anxiety for several months, especially more than six months.

- If you have seen signs of anxiety that have recurred in several stages of her development.
- If your daughter's self-esteem has been impacted by anxiety to the degree that you feel like she's showing signs of withdrawal and even depression.
- If you see her suffering across the primary areas of her life: home, school, and friendships.
- If she's no longer able to go to school.
- If anxiety prevents her from doing the things she loves most.
- If she is affected physically to the point that she's truly sick and her pediatrician has said there's no physical cause.

Whatever the situation is, whatever degree of worry your daughter is facing, I assure you she can work through it. Just as I've seen an anxiety epidemic in my office, I've also seen thousands of girls who have beaten their Worry Monsters.

I know that you're ready for her to be free of her worries. I can assure you she is too. Children want to be independent. She not only wants you to feel proud of her, she wants to feel proud of herself. But, remember, especially if she's anxious, she underestimates herself. She needs help. She needs you to understand not only what's happening to her, but why. (Hint: It's really for reasons that speak to the bravery and strength and intelligence that are already inside of her. But she doesn't know that yet.) In the meantime, she needs you to believe in her. She needs you to remind her often that she's capable. And she needs you to give her opportunities to prove it.

Key Points to Remember

- We all have hundreds of intrusive thoughts daily. Kids don't say those thoughts out loud for fear someone will think something is wrong with them.
- Girls tend to blame themselves for things. Because of this and their desire for relationship, girls, in particular, struggle with voicing their worries out loud.
- Fear, worry, and anxiety all exist on the same continuum.
- Fears are a normal part of her growing up. In fact, there are typical fears children face at different stages of their development. The passage of those fears has to do with two primary factors: experience and trust.
- Worry is more conceptual than fear. Fears turn to worry when the evidence increases the likelihood of the scary thing happening.
- Children develop their own strategies for dealing with worry.
- Anxiety is a state of perpetual worry and constant pressure.
- Anxiety, left untreated, only gets worse.
- Anxiety always involves an overestimation of the problem and an underestimation of herself.
- Anxiety is born out of fear but has a reaction that is disproportionate to the fear.
- For some children, counseling and even medication are needed to work through their level of anxiety. This does not mean that you're not helping as a parent. It just means you need a bigger, more specifically trained team.
- Your daughter can beat the Worry Monster. She needs you to remind her and give her opportunities.
- The more you and she learn about her worries, the weaker they get. The more she listens to them, the stronger they become.

Understanding Yourself and Your Daughter Better

What have you realized about your daughter after reading this chapter?

What have you realized about yourself?

Do you have looping thoughts? Does your daughter? What are those thoughts about?

Do you believe she leans more toward fears, worry, or anxiety?

Have you ever struggled with anxiety, based on this chapter's descriptions?

If so, how old were you, and what was your anxiety centered on?

Does your child overestimate threats?

Does she underestimate herself?

Do you struggle with either of these concepts?

What do you want for her, having read the pages of this chapter?

Where do you see your daughter as capable and strong?

When could you take an opportunity to remind her of those things?

2. Why Her?

I got a text from a friend this week who knew I was working on this book. "Here's the deal," she said. "We want to know (1) How we can help our kids, and (2) What we did to cause this problem. We're all feeling a lot of mom guilt over here."

I do *not* want you to be reading this book with, or out of, mom guilt or dad guilt or anyone guilt. If your daughter is a worrier or has anxiety, I know you may be asking yourself, "Why her?" She is very likely asking herself, "Why me?"

Let me tell you what I say to every girl facing anxiety: "You feel this way because you're really great. The smartest, most conscientious, try-hard, care-about-things girls I know are the ones who struggle with anxiety. It's honestly because you're awesome. You care so much, and that's the bottom line of why you worry."

I'm serious—let's start there. The girls I see who live with anxiety are some of the most hardworking, caring, intentional, kind, brilliant girls I know. Things matter to them. *Everything* matters to them, which can make life hard. And it can make it hard to know when or how to turn that kind of care off.

Also, it's helpful for her to know she's in good company. I tell girls that anxiety is the primary mental health problem among children and teens.[1] Not that I would use the phrase "mental health" in my office with girls themselves, necessarily. That sounds like the catastrophizing we're going to be talking more about later. But it does help her a *lot* to know she's not the only one struggling. I explain it more like, "I talk to girls every day who worry more than they wish they would. They have trouble turning those good brains of theirs off, and so they have lots of looping thoughts. And believe me, I have heard girls say they're worried about everything you can imagine. There is nothing you could say that would surprise me or make me think less of you."

So, let's talk about the good and prevalent company she is keeping. Here are some anxiety-related statistics:

- Anxiety is the primary mental health problem facing children and teens today and has been so for more than a decade.[2]
- Anxiety is also the primary mental health problem for adults.[3]
- Half of adults who report anxiety say that their anxiety began when they were children.[4]
- Although they may appear earlier, symptoms have been known to emerge in children as young as four or five years of age.[5]
- Statistics show that one in five children develops an anxiety disorder, and many more will be on the outskirts of that statistic.[6]
- Affluent children and teens are at especially high risk of developing anxiety disorders.[7]
- Today's teens and young adults are five to eight times more likely to experience symptoms of anxiety disorders than people were in history, including during events such as the Great Depression, World War II, and the Cold War.[8]
- Untreated anxiety in children is one of the greatest predictors of depression during adolescence and adulthood.[9]
- The average span of time a child experiences anxiety before beginning therapy is two years.[10]

According to the National Institute of Mental Health, "An estimated 31.1% of U.S. adults experience any anxiety disorder at some time in their lives."[11] What that means is that more than one-fourth of your friends, colleagues, and neighbors battle anxiety. One out of every five students in your daughter's class will not only struggle with anxiety but will develop an anxiety disorder. And there are differences in the rates of boys and of girls—in the prevalence of anxiety (as well as the treatment of it).

By adolescence, girls are twice as likely to develop an anxiety disorder as boys.[12] Boys, however, says Dr. Tamar Chansky, are brought in for treatment more than girls.[13] Why? What is going on with girls?

The Pressure Girls Face

Leonard Sax says, "More and more boys are developing an epicurean ability to enjoy themselves—to enjoy video games, pornography, food, and sleep—but they often don't have the drive and motivation to succeed in the real world outside their bedroom. More and more of their sisters have that drive and motivation in abundance—but they don't know how to relax, have fun, and enjoy life."[14]

Remember, girls are much more likely to skew things against themselves. The problem lies inside of them, and so they need to work harder and do better in most everything. The tragedy is that they're working harder without as much input or assistance. Sax goes on to say, "There has never before been any culture in which girls have had so many opportunities and yet received so little structured guidance."[15]

Just Because She Can...

Your worried girl is also likely a dependable one. If she's old enough and you have younger children, you know she will take care of them if you leave her in charge. She can get her homework done on her own, whereas you have to check on her brother repeatedly. You sure wouldn't ask *him* to fix her lunch for school, but she is capable, after all. She's responsible. She's conscientious. She's also feeling an immense amount of pressure.

Because these girls can do most everything, we often expect them to do it all. And, what I've found in my office is that parents are typically harder on the firstborn of their same gender. So, moms, I would respectfully guess that you expect a lot from her. To help with her younger siblings. To keep her room clean. To be a role model. To be respectful and kind and friendly and make good grades and do her chores.

She wants to please you. Even when she's older and it's hard to tell past the preadolescent eye rolls, she still wants to please you. She doesn't want to let you down. She doesn't want to let her teacher down. She doesn't want to let her friends down. And she really hates to fail.

We're also living in a time when the talk is that girls can do anything, which is fantastic in so many ways. Academics. Athletics. Leadership positions. Service. The arts. Relationships. Girls didn't have the opportunities when we were growing up to be involved in as many things as they do now. But knowing *they can* sometimes translates to feeling like they have to. **Opportunity becomes expectation, in their eyes.** Sometimes we push them because "we never had the chance to do those things when we were younger," but they also often push themselves. I have sat with hundreds of parents over the years who've told me that their daughters set higher expectations for themselves than they ever could set for them. But those expectations are still often born out of a desire to please.

"Girls beat out boys in college and graduate school admissions," CNN writer Rachel Simmons says, but "according to a University of California–Los Angeles study, female college freshmen have never been lonelier or less happy."[16] As one girl said to me recently in counseling, "It's all just too much. It's like I have too many choices and too many opportunities with what I want to do with my life. I'm just still trying to figure out who I am. I feel like I have all of the insight in the world, but I have no idea what to do with it. It's really overwhelming."

Do you feel the pressure yet, just reading about this? Girls have a perfect storm brewing inside of and around them. They're afraid to fail. They care deeply. They are capable and conscientious. They have every opportunity in front of them. They expect a lot of themselves. We sometimes expect a lot of them. And, in turn, they want us to value them and delight in them . . . and they want every relationship that comes after us to do the same. And this is all before they ever reach the age of eight.

Actually, in 2010, a study in *Pediatrics* journal reported that 15 percent of girls were starting puberty by the age of seven, says psychotherapist Allison Edwards in her book *Why Smart Kids Worry*.[17] So, not only do they have all of the pressure around them, they've got emotions and hormones swirling around inside of them, too, that are confusing and overwhelming. Girls mature faster than boys, and with that maturity comes an emotional sensitivity. In essence, their emotions are outrunning their ability to process those emotions. It's not clear why this is happening faster than ever before, but one researcher commented, "Over the last thirty years, we've shortened the childhood of girls by a year and a half."[18]

And then there's body image. The following statistics are from the Body Image Therapy Center and a report by eating disorder specialist Heather Gallivan.

- 89% of girls have dieted by age seventeen[19]
- 15% of young women have disordered eating[20]
- 42% of girls in grades one to three want to lose weight[21]
- 45% of girls in grades three to six want to be thinner[22]
- 51% of nine- and ten-year-old girls say they feel better about themselves when they are dieting[23]
- 80% of ten-year-olds fear being fat[24]

- 53% of thirteen-year-old girls are unhappy with their bodies[25]
- 78% of seventeen-year-old girls are unhappy with their bodies[26]

Girls feel too much pressure—to please, to perform, to excel, to be responsible. Plus, they want to look beautiful while they're doing it all, and doing it all well. They feel pressure before they're really old enough to understand it. They don't yet have the skills to cope, which is where we come in.

We need to be helping girls value the process more than success. We want them to focus on effort they can control, rather than on an outcome they can't. **We need to encourage girls more for their effort than the outcome.** We need to celebrate partial successes. We need to talk about our own failures and laugh at our own mistakes. We need to arm them with tools to battle not only their worries, but the pressures they encounter from within and without on a daily basis. And we need to help them with one of the biggest pressures we never had to face growing up: technology.

The Tension of Technology

These days, Snapchat and Instagram are the primary ways girls communicate. Girls are acutely aware of the number of followers and "likes" on everything they do. If a girl doesn't get enough "likes" on the photo she posts on Instagram, she takes it down. In other words, or, maybe we should say, in her words: "If I don't get enough approval, whatever I experienced isn't valid." She doesn't necessarily say that out loud, but it's what is happening. The pressure is to post enough to keep people interested, but not enough to make people annoyed. Plus, girls feel they need to stand the right way, smile just enough, look pretty, pose with the "right" people, and have a clever caption, all at the same time. Just this week a seventh-grade girl told me that, at a sleepover with a friend, they spent three hours trying to come up with the perfect caption for a photo. Three hours. They ended up not posting the photo because they couldn't figure it out. How's that for pressure?

Regarding Snapchat, one of the biggest trends of the moment is Snapstreaks. I recently had a conversation with another middle school girl about "streaks," as teens call them. Actually, she had a conversation with me, because I was having a hard time understanding the concept—or maybe just the reasoning behind it.

"I only have like ten streaks going, but a lot of my friends have thirty," she told me. A streak is when you send a message or photo to each other every day for a given number of days. "Some people have streaks for one hundred days. I know a girl who has had a streak for six hundred days with someone." (In case you're wondering, that's one year, seven months, and three weeks. I didn't even know streaks had been around that long.) "Basically," she went on to say, "if you don't have a streak going with someone, it means you don't like them."

When I asked her how long it took her just to respond to her streaks, she said, "Anywhere from thirty minutes to an hour. It's kind of hard with homework and sports practices. But I sure don't want my friends to think I'm mad at them. And I can't stop the streak!" Her last sentence to me, when I asked how streaks benefited her friendships, was "I guess they don't. But I don't know what would happen to my relationships if I didn't keep them going. I'm afraid I'd lose them."

Snapchat streaks? I can't even call people back on a daily basis, let alone keep up with thirty social media messages back and forth. Can you see the pressure these kids live under? I talked to a parent recently who kept up her daughter's streaks while she was on a month-long mission trip because the girl was so worried about dropping the streaks.

By the time you read this, there will likely be a new social media platform that has come up with even more pressure-filled ways to keep the girls we love engaged (and engaged constantly). They'll be even more aware of the parties they're missing and the get-togethers they're being excluded from, all of which contribute to the anxiety and depression I see daily in my office. Interestingly, I read a study recently that said girls reported that social media is not contributing to their anxiety or depression. This is not what girls tell me behind the closed doors of my counseling office.

We could talk at length about the tension they, and we, feel about technology, but it would take up this entire book. Suffice it to say, I believe that kids need to gradually learn responsible technology use. They earn more privileges when they prove themselves responsible and as they mature more emotionally. We want to go slow and hold off on allowing them to use technology on their own for as long as we can, knowing that technology is the primary way they communicate. But it also is a significant contributing factor to the anxiety we see girls deal with daily.

The technology-related anxiety starts early, though, and it's not just a result of social media. A physician told me recently that just the barrage of stimulation on a screen—the constant images and sounds—creates a heightened state of arousal in kids' brains. When they live in this heightened state for too long or too often, the brain has a hard time calming itself back down. Again, we could talk about technology and its impact on girls in so many ways. The bottom line is that it is furthering their anxiety. They need us to help them learn to use technology responsibly and appropriately, which is extremely hard in the face of this pressure. But they sure need us to try.

Fifteen years ago, I taught one of my first parenting seminars on raising girls. I'll never forget the dad who walked up to me afterward and said, "I can't wait to go home and tell my girls I had no idea how hard it was to be a girl." I love that dad's heart and his desire to communicate and connect with his girls.

It *is* hard to be a girl. But their parents trying to understand them and their worlds can help alleviate their worries. Talk to your daughter. Ask her questions about the pressure she feels outside and inside of her. Ask her about the culture of her school and about the tension she feels around technology. And then go have fun with her. Help her get back to the relaxing and playing and enjoying life that Leonard Sax talked about in the beginning of the chapter. It would be good for you both, and for your relationship.

Profiles of an Anxious Girl

We've established that girls are battling worries and anxiety more than ever, but as mentioned earlier, they are coming in for treatment less. Why?

Laura came in for counseling at the age of twelve, but her worries had started much earlier. Her mom showed me a photo from Laura's sixth birthday party. Laura's younger sister had her arm around Laura and was laughing. Laura, on the other hand, was crying over her cake. Her mom looked at me standing over the picture, smiled, and said, "It started early with her." She described Laura as compliant, kind, sensitive, and shy. She was the oldest child of four. She didn't make friends easily as an introvert, but she did have a few close friends in elementary school. In middle school, friendships got more difficult. Most days she came home from school disheartened and discouraged by experiences with peers. She felt like she couldn't connect and drifted further and further away from even trying. Her parents reassured and coaxed and tried to cheer her on, but nothing was working. And so they brought Laura in to see me.

Sophia came in for counseling when she was seven. Sophia was the youngest in her family—and also the most impulsive. She was boisterous, a little aggressive, and a lot of fun. She was getting into trouble at home and was starting to get into trouble at school. She played with the boys on the playground more than with the girls, and her parents were becoming concerned. Maybe even more than concerned, they were tired. "We're wondering if she has ADHD. She has outbursts of anger. She has trouble focusing in class. She gets furious at us and says things without thinking. And the girls in class don't seem to want to be around her." Honestly, I also wondered if Sophia could have some type of attention deficit hurdle.

She was impulsive, struggled to focus in school, and was also missing social cues, which happens to be an indicator in many girls for attention-deficit/hyperactivity disorder (ADHD). When she was tested, however, she registered much higher on anxiety than on any kind of attention hurdle.

As a side note, if you believe your child might be battling clinical anxiety or ADHD, or a wide variety of learning or psychological hurdles, testing can be a profoundly helpful tool. I tell parents regularly that testing fast-forwards the therapeutic process significantly. For example, ADHD and anxiety can look very similar symptomatically but are very different in methodology of treatment. Therefore, it gives counselors an earlier and wider scope of understanding in what will be most helpful with your child. Neuropsychological testing is done by a licensed clinical psychologist. Your pediatrician can be a great referral source for a trusted psychological testing location.

Ella is a junior in high school. She makes good grades. She goes on mission trips on her spring and summer breaks to foreign countries where she works in orphanages. She's an officer in the National Honor Society and one of the girls in her youth group who tries to help all of the new girls feel comfortable. She is a delight to be around. And it's all coming at great cost. She's overwhelmed and teary any time she slows down. She's starting to show signs of depression, although she covers it up well with work and smiles. According to Ella, her anxiety is what keeps her going. But she has no idea of the real toll it's taking on her heart.

Emma came to see me because she was having stomachaches every day at school. She came home early a lot. She had been to the pediatrician three times, and there was nothing physically wrong. He directed her family to Daystar. Emma had a really hard time talking about her feelings. She had a huge smile and seemed to be more Tigger than Eeyore. She was beloved by her teachers at school and her friends, too, according to her mom. But the more we talked, the more it was clear that Emma didn't feel loved. She was really sensitive. She watched and took in a great deal and felt even the smallest slight from one of her friends as a huge rupture in their relationship. She felt deeply, and those feelings were all coming out through her tummy.

Victoria was ten years old and very quiet. You could barely hear her little voice when she talked. She usually wanted her mom to come up with her when she came to my office and was reluctant to let her mom leave halfway through the session. Victoria was fearful and extremely rigid. She confessed every "bad" thought or feeling she ever had. She had a difficult time letting go of those thoughts and also had a difficult time with choices and transitions. Before school and bedtime were her most difficult times of the day. She had meltdowns about what to wear in the mornings and had a hard time falling asleep for rehearsing all of the things she felt she had done wrong throughout her day. Victoria and her parents were exhausted.

For the most part, the anxiety Victoria and the other girls experience lies just under the surface. Or it lies under what we think of as introversion, or perfectionism, or even ADHD tendencies. An anxious girl may avoid sports for fear of letting down the team. Maybe she avoids friends for fear of saying the wrong thing and has fewer as a result. Maybe she has trouble falling asleep or spends excessive time trying to get her homework just right. Maybe she washes her hands continually or asks you a million questions, seeking reassurance.

Worry looks different on every girl. And on every parent. But most parents of girls who worry come into my offices saying something like, "That's just the way she is" or "She's always been this way." The parents all, however, feel worried and weary. The girls all feel like things aren't quite right . . . and, in their minds, it's likely because something is wrong with them. And the pressure and worries inside of them just keep building, but they're without the tools to cope.

One helpful tool that is also featured in the activity book *Braver, Stronger, Smarter* is what I call a worry thermometer. I want her (and you) to take your "worry temperature" on a scale of sorts that shows how intense that worry feels at any given moment. What's your worry level currently? What would you guess hers is?

As I mentioned before, girls who worry often have outsides that don't match their insides. Their worry goes up the thermometer, and rather than saying, "I'm worried, Mom" or "I feel a little anxious, Dad; can you help?" they explode in anger. (Remember, they don't have the words or tools yet to do something different.) Or they implode in tears and shame or just simply shrink back. Most girls—most of us—lean one way or the other. We process our worries and anxiety externally or internally, and your daughter's worry profile will have to do with which way she leans.

The Exploders

Exploders' worries come out. They wouldn't necessarily be labeled as anxious by their teachers or their parents. They're more likely to be labeled as angry or attention seeking or just plain trouble. Especially in young children, their acting-out behavior is much easier to see than any kind of worry that might be inside of them. Their feelings are exaggerated. They yell. They get frustrated with you, but even more frustrated with themselves. They let you know it. In fact, for an external worry processor, you become their primary coping skill. In other words, they have huge feelings. They don't know what to do with the feelings. And you just happen to be standing nearby. You also happen to be safe and will love them no matter what. And so exploders explode. They scream and cry and tell you that "YOU'RE NOT DOING IT RIGHT!"

The thing is, the real reason her ponytail "isn't right" is because she's worried about the birthday party and if she'll know what to say or how to talk to her friends. You're not doing the math right, because she feels panicky about keeping up her good grades and pleasing her teacher.

Exploders feel like they need to be in control. They become rigid when things feel out of control. When they get rigid, their worry gets stronger and their emotions get even bigger. Their explosions are like a release valve. They function out of the fight-or-flight region of their brain, but often don't feel like they can really fight with anyone other than you. They feel better when the explosion is over, but you feel worse. And, usually at some point, they do, too, and come to you in tears, apologizing. They might even apologize over and over because exploders often tend to over-confess.

Can you guess which of our girls described earlier is an exploder? You got it: Sophia. Sophia is a classic exploder. She tries to keep her worries pushed down, but she is impulsive enough that they shoot out anyway. She has trouble focusing in class, but not because her brain can't focus. It's that her brain is so busy focusing on her worries that there's no time to focus on schoolwork.

Victoria is also an exploder. But she's quiet until she explodes. Both girls use their parents as their primary coping method. Their emotions go up the worry scale. They try to process them externally—which mostly involves yelling. (As grown-ups, we call this venting.) But the yelling, or loud, emotionally elevated talking, only makes things worse for everyone involved. The girls and their parents need tools to help them find other more constructive and less hurtful coping skills. We've got those coming in the next section.

The Imploders

Exploders turn on someone else, but imploders turn mostly on themselves. Laura, Ella, and Emma are all examples of imploders. They minimize their feelings and then blame themselves for those feelings. Meanwhile, the feelings often have physical expressions. Their bodies tell the tale with stomachaches or headaches.

On the outside, imploders often look like model children, and so we miss their worry too. They smile and try hard, even if they do tend to step behind you a little when you're speaking to people after church. They're typically some of the best students, although they find raising their hands intimidating. It's not that they don't know the answer. It's that they're so worried about others and blaming themselves that they think there is a great likelihood their right answer will be wrong and they'll look foolish.

Imploders want to be in control too. But rather than trying to outwardly maintain control and then exploding when they don't have it, they hang back. They avoid the situation that makes them feel out of control. And they become masters at hiding those feelings. In the meantime, the feelings have to come out, in one way or another.

I sat with a dad recently who assured me that his twelve-year-old daughter was fine, despite the fact that she was washing her hands more than twenty times a day. No one really knew what was going on inside of her, although her mom had a sneaking suspicion that something wasn't quite right. The girl was pleasant, getting good grades, and respectful of all of the adults in her life. But, again, her outsides did not match what was happening inside. She seemed "fine" when she walked into my counseling office, just as her dad said. You may have heard that FINE is an acronym for Feelings in Need of Expression, which was exactly what was going on with her. Her feelings weren't coming out directly, but they were coming out through compulsive hand washing. She needed other tools. Her coping skills were hurting her more than others, which was exactly how she intended it. But the hurt was hard to detect, as is the case with so many girls who worry.

Temperament Indicators

There's a great chance that the temperament of this girl, from the time she was little, had been pointing toward worry tendencies. Harvard psychology professor Jerome Kagan has done a great deal of research around the temperament of children. *New York Times* reporter Robin Marantz Henig writes that Kagan believes some children are "wired to worry" from as young as four months old. These children showed a strong reaction to "novel people or situations." And, based on longitudinal studies out of Harvard and several other research groups, babies with strong reactions grow up to be anxious teenagers and adults. They have what's referred to as a hyperreactive amygdala, which is the fight-or-flight region of the brain that we'll talk much more about in the "Help" section. As a result, he said that 15 to 20 percent of children are more predisposed to anxiety than others.[27]

We also see a tendency in our counseling practice toward anxiety in children who are naturally gifted. It has partly to do with their inherent strengths: keen observation and advanced cognitive processing, higher levels of emotional sensitivity and empathy, and active imaginations. Because these children can also be quite literal, perfectionistic, and concrete in their thinking, they sometimes have mental competencies that surpass their social competencies. Their intelligence becomes their identity, and competition and a sense of being right can overpower the importance of being kind. At that point, they're aware enough to realize that they interact with the world differently but can't move past their own giftedness to relate to other children. The discrepancies in their levels of maturity and difficulties in connection in turn lead to increased anxiety in these gifted children.

The "Chicken Little" temperaments of the world also seem predisposed toward anxiety. Children who not only skew things negatively against themselves, but skew things negatively in general, struggle with worry more than other children do. They not only believe the sky is falling, but it's likely going to fall on them. Psychologists call this a negativity bias. A negativity bias means that we not only see the negative more quickly, but we also feel its impact more strongly. In other words, we find what we're looking for, and then it hurts. Then, Chicken Little creates a chicken-or-the-egg type of situation.

When a child (or adult) is negative, they tend to see the negative around them more and then feel more negatively about the world. Negativity begets negativity begets anxiety. And, for this child, they're "always left out," they "never get picked first" for the team, the teacher "always calls on the other kids more," and they're "never included when the other kids hang out." The negativity bias leads to more isolation and more anxiety in a child who was potentially predisposed that way in the first place. And the even greater problem is that we fall for it. Stay tuned for more on that one.

Experiential Factors

"In this world you will have trouble." —John 16:33

It's the verse we're going to come back to throughout the final chapters of this book. You know hard things are going to happen in the life of your child, as much as you wish you could prevent them. She'll have hard days at school when friends are mean to her or leave her out. There will be hurt between family members, such as when a sibling calls her names. You will inevitably blow it and hurt her too. Those are all pieces of life in a fallen world and living with and loving other sinners. We fail each other daily, and it hurts.

As a counselor, I believe it's never been more important to talk about how the trouble your child will experience can lead to resilience. In fact, children are immunized against stress by handling stressful situations. We want her to learn how she can see difficulties as opportunities. And, ultimately, how God can and will use hurt in her life—even big hurt—for her good and His glory. That's going to be a lesson we circle back to over and over in this book, and you will circle back to it throughout her life. Those experiences of hurt, however, can also create anxiety, especially when they're more of what we would refer to as trauma.

There is a great deal of talk around trauma in today's culture. It is reported that more than two-thirds of children today experience a traumatic event by age sixteen.[28] Trauma is defined by the American Psychological Association as "an emotional response to a terrible event like an accident, rape or natural disaster."[29] After trauma, sufferers may experience extreme sadness, anger, post-traumatic stress disorder (which is an anxiety-related disorder we talk about in Appendix 1), or other physical, mental, and emotional issues related to the trauma.

The jury is still out on the exact correlation between trauma and anxiety. Clinical psychologist Bridget Flynn Walker says there is no empirical data to suggest any definitive causation.[30] However, author Tamar Chansky writes, "A child who has experienced a traumatic event is twice as likely to develop some type of difficulty—whether anxiety, depression, or a behavioral disorder." Chansky adds that "many studies suggest that the majority of children who undergo trauma do recover without incident."[31]

In my practice, I've seen it go both ways. I've seen children experience what is often referred to now as a "little *t* trauma," such as mild bullying or a family move, and come through stronger for it. I've seen girls in the very same situation who have shrunk back and lost their voice. I've seen children who have lived through what is often called a "big *T* trauma," such as the loss of a sibling or parent, and experienced a debilitating anxiety for years that created a darkness so pervasive they couldn't see their own way out. And I've seen children who have experienced similar tragedy and grieved deeply but continued to move forward in a way that created more resilience rather than more trauma. What I've concluded is that much of a child's response to trauma has to do with ours.

Our brains struggle to process traumatic events. They become overwhelmed with the shock and the pain, and so the memories become chaotic and fragmented. As a result, the memories aren't stored like other memories, and we relive those memories in dreams and flashbacks, often accompanied by emotional, mental, and physical distress. This is true for adults whose brains are fully developed, so you can imagine the impact trauma has on a brain that's not yet fully formed.

It is imperative that we provide children the help they need when they have undergone trauma, whether that trauma is the little or big T type. They need you to be a safe place where they can talk, and they often need help finding their way to a professional who can help them make sense of the experience in a therapeutic way.

This past summer, we had one of the most moving mornings I remember at Hopetown, our counseling version of a summer retreat program. The fifth- and sixth-graders talked about different struggles they had gone through, sharing both tears and hope. One girl hung around after the other kids had gone to lunch and wanted to talk. She had come to Daystar when her older brother was killed a few months before in a car accident, and, as you can imagine, she was still grieving deeply. We talked for a while, and she cried a good bit, more than she ever had before with me. After about twenty minutes, her closest Hopetown friend walked up and asked if she could talk with us. I turned to the other girl, who, through her tears, smiled and said, "Absolutely." So, this second girl sat down and said, "I wanted to tell you both about my dad. I've never told anyone, but he's in prison." The girl who lost her brother stood up, put her arms around her, and said, "I can't even imagine how hard that's been for you." I was blown away. These girls were in the sixth grade. How many adults do we know who would have been irritated by the second girl even interrupting the conversation, who would have had a difficult time with the attention shifting off them, or who would have had no idea what to say? It felt like Genesis 50:20 walked out right in front of me: What the enemy meant for evil, God meant for good. God was using the pain from the first girl's experience to show profound compassion and empathy to her friend. She was working through her big T trauma, largely with the help of her parents and counseling.

Your daughter will experience trouble, pain, and possibly even trauma this side of heaven. But you are instrumental in how that trouble translates. The combination of you, God, and the right help can turn that trouble into good eventually. There is always hope.

Profiles of an Anxious Parent

After reading the last few pages, what are you feeling? What temperature is your worry thermometer at now?

Look back to the last sentence of the previous section: There is always hope. I want you to hold on to that statement. No matter what has happened in her life or yours, no matter what part of the anxiety has a genetic component, no matter what unintentional mistakes you've made in your parenting journey, **there is always hope.** It's a journey. And not only are you and she still on it, but God is still going before you in it. We say the same four words in every parenting seminar we ever teach: "*It's never too late.*"

So, here's the deal. You heard it already: One of the biggest predictors of anxiety in kids is anxiety in parents. (But don't forget that there's still hope . . . it's never too late!) We're going to talk about how and why and what you can do to turn the tide for your daughter today.

The Genetics

The way that we do our intake appointments at Daystar always follows the same pattern. I walk into the lobby and introduce myself to the child and their parent(s). Then I say to that child, "Let me give you a tour, and then we'll go talk for a few minutes. After that, I'll come bring you back down, and we'll swap, and I'll talk to your parents for a little bit." I then proceed to give her a tour around the office, complete with snacks and water and introductions to our resident therapy dogs. Then we go sit down in my office to talk. We always meet with the child first, because we want them to feel like Daystar is *their* safe place.

In that initial meeting, many children tell me that they struggle with worry. They tell me why their parents wanted them to come, and often how their parents explained counseling to them (which is always interesting to hear). I've been called a "feelings doctor" more times than I can count, although there is no doctor anywhere attached to my name. (Still, it's a great idea if you ever take your little one to counseling.) Then after we talk for a few minutes, I take the child back down to the lobby and bring the parent(s) up. "Tell me about your daughter," the conversation starts. And, you guessed it, in keeping with the statistics, a majority of those conversations center around the girl's anxiety.

Now, have you ever had a conversation with someone who's really anxious? It's obvious fairly quickly. Anxiety seems to have a pervasive quality. I start to feel anxious when I'm with really anxious people. I've had countless times when I've sat with parents who describe their concerns for an anxious daughter. And then, when I ask, "Do you happen to have any family history of anxiety?" they'll say, "No! None at all."

Children of anxious parents are as much as seven times more likely to develop an anxiety disorder than children who don't have anxious parents, according to a study by researchers at Johns Hopkins University.[32] In their book *Anxious Kids, Anxious Parents*, psychologist Reid Wilson and psychotherapist Lynn Lyons report that "up to 65 percent of children living with an anxious parent meet the criteria for an anxiety disorder."[33] Based on these and numerous twin studies, researchers have been able to determine that anxiety is, in fact, inheritable. But, according to Chansky, genetics only determines 30–40 percent of the anxiety we're seeing today, with the rest related to environment and the factors we discussed in the last section.[34]

The research also points out that a parent who isn't anxious is of extreme benefit to a child when the other parent is anxious, say Wilson and Lyons. However, it also states that the nonanxious parent's opinion is often dismissed as careless or not attentive enough.[35] Both of your voices are important, and his or her lack of anxiety helps to even out the effect of your anxiety.

You may not know if your daughter's anxiety is inherited. Many parents have no idea. I'll just go ahead and tell on myself. I don't feel anxious on a daily basis. But I'm a classic type A personality—a one on the Enneagram. The older I get, the more I come to believe individuals who are type A deal with a little (or a lot of) baseline anxiety. And our productivity, efficiency, and organization are all systems to keep our worlds in control. They're how we manage our anxiety or keep it at bay so it doesn't take over. They're how we make our worlds work. So, if you happen to join me in the well-ordered ranks of being type A, I want you to include yourself (and I will too) in this category.

I recently read an article called "If You Have These 7 Habits, You Might Have High-Functioning Anxiety."[36] (HFA doesn't impede day-to-day activities). You ready?

1. You can't sleep.
2. You pay close attention to details.
3. You can't relax.
4. You engage in "numbing" behaviors [which could include exercise, TV, or a LOT of other things we all do every day].
5. You focus on control.
6. You push yourself to your limits.
7. You plan everything.

I'm wondering if the writer has ever met a parent? Ummm . . . welcome to every day of your life as a mom or dad. Every one of those things is part of what it looks like to raise tiny humans. But I want you to consider them. Think about your own level of worry. Or even anxiety. I also want you to spend a few minutes thinking about your parents. Your grandparents. Did they seem fearful? What about overly controlling? Did they seem to have a conspiracy-theory-type view of life? Were they overprotective of you? Are you showing any of those types of behavior toward your daughter currently? If your child is struggling with worry, these are important questions. If you or another family member has had anxiety, she's significantly more likely to struggle with it herself from a genetic standpoint. But if you or another parent has anxiety, you also may be unwittingly setting her up to struggle from an environmental perspective as well.

Modeling

Genetics predispose us to certain behaviors. If you have a family member who is an alcoholic, for example, that doesn't mean that you'll become an alcoholic yourself. It does mean that the chances are higher that you could, if given the right set of circumstances. With alcohol, however, you can stay away from a bar your entire life. With anxiety, the deck gets stacked a little more.

Your brain and your child's brain have something called "mirror neurons." Neurons are cells in the brain that activate when we either perform an action or watch an action being performed. Mirror neurons are what enabled your daughter to learn to tie her shoes as she watched you tie yours. It's how she learns to shoot a basket and water-ski. It's how you learned to cook. It's also one of the ways anxiety can be contagious.

In fact, mirror neurons begin their work in her earliest stages. In their book *The Self-Driven Child*, clinical neuropsychologist William Stixrud and motivational coach Ned Johnson write, "When parents of newborns are stressed, the babies cry and fuss more than if their parents are feeling calm and confident."[37] And it just keeps going. When you wring your hands in worry over your daughter's first day at school or when you pace back and forth before her first piano recital, her mirror neurons jump into gear. They not only fire as if they were performing those actions, but they also take on the stress that your brain and your level of worry are giving off. Mirror neurons are one reason why, in our book *Are My Kids on Track?*, my friend David says that children "learn more through observation than information."[38]

Children mirror their parents' actions. Their neurons mirror your neurons. But they also hear the words you use when you're fearful and watch how you approach your own challenges. In a study including mothers who struggle with some degree of social anxiety, researchers found that those mothers "make more catastrophic" and "threat-related comments" than nonanxious mothers, according to the authors of *Parent-Led CBT for Child Anxiety*. In other words, they have big reactions and use big words to describe a threat, overestimating the problem and underestimating themselves.[39] Of course, children who want to be like their parents will not only use that same language, but take on the same perspective that their parents are modeling for them.

Parenting Styles

Genetics predispose us to certain behaviors. That behavior, in front of the children we love, is called modeling. When repeated over time, that behavior becomes a parenting style. In other words, when you have anxiety, you act and live in an anxious way, sometimes even when you don't mean to. You model anxious behavior, and you eventually develop what could be called an anxious parenting style.

Wall Street Journal writer Andrea Peterson says research shows that two of the primary types of parenting styles associated with anxiety in children are overprotection and overcontrol.[40] Overprotection and overcontrol come from two potentially different motivations, but their effect on the girls we love is much the same.

With overprotection, a parent has often experienced anxiety themselves, likely in their own childhood. "I don't want her to feel like I did" is the sentence this parent would say to me in my office. They don't want their child to feel paralyzing fear. They want her to feel confident and strong instead. And so they try to keep her out of situations that create those feelings of fear or inadequacy. In other words, they rescue, they fix, they help her avoid the situations that trigger the fear.

But here's the thing: When you rescue her, you're communicating to her that she needs rescuing. You're telling her the situation is a frightening one and she's not capable of handling it. (Remember overestimating the problem and underestimating herself? We just accidentally reinforced those very messages.) In essence, you're inadvertently encouraging her dependence on you, rather than her independence. And as we said before, all children long to be independent. Just because you processed your anxiety in a certain way doesn't mean that she'll process hers the same. She wants independence. And, in fact, she needs it.

A friend of mine, Paris Goodyear-Brown, is a respected anxiety therapist and author of *The Worry Wars*. She came and spoke to our staff on kids and worry. The bottom line of her entire talk was that "for kids to work through anxiety, they just have to do the scary thing anyway." (Did your worry thermometer shoot up just now?) We're going to talk lots more about this in the next section of the book and give you practical ideas for how to support your daughter in doing the scary thing. But, I will say, when you overprotect her, your fear often has more to do with you than it does with her. I see anxious parents weekly whose children "aren't ready" to do a certain task. In actuality, it's the parent who's not ready . . . because of their own fear that the child will be hurt. But it's in this world that they have trouble, and that trouble is where they find opportunities to grow.

In addition, overprotecting doesn't work. It doesn't take away kids' fear. A study cited in *Parent-Led CBT for Child Anxiety* found that children whose parents were more involved with a child's assigned presentation ended up being even more anxious when the time came to give the presentation.[41] They still have to do the scary thing. Children who are rescued end up needing to be rescued more and also have the side benefit of getting attention from you during the rescuing. A teenage girl told me recently that she felt closer to her mom when she had panic attacks than any other time, so "maybe I let myself get really anxious because that's the time she's most nurturing to me."

Now, let's talk about the overcontrollers. Overcontrollers also end up overprotecting, but they often step in because they believe their children aren't capable. They don't want them to feel fear. But they also don't want them to fail. Maybe the daughter struggles with ADHD combined with her anxiety, or maybe she struggles socially, or she acts out in school. Honestly, it's also sometimes that this parent just can't help themselves. They don't necessarily want to be controlling, but they think things will likely fall apart if they're not.

It doesn't work, either, does it? If we solve our kids' problems for them, they don't develop the ability to problem-solve, which I believe is one of the primary deterrents of anxiety. A 2006 study at University of California, Los Angeles found that parents who intervene in tasks their children are performing or could perform on their own, not only limit their child's ability to perform the task successfully but also cause greater separation anxiety in that particular child.[42] Another study found that parents who were told that their children might struggle over a puzzle task intervened more than parents who were told their child would find it fun.[43]

We worry. We think children might struggle or aren't capable, and we step in. When we step in, they step out—or check out or lean on us. It's a self-fulfilling prophecy. We end up solving the problem because we don't believe they're capable. They never learn to solve the problem, and so they are incapable. And then we become more controlling, and sometimes more critical, in the process. Another study found that parents with social anxiety not only expressed more doubt in their children's abilities, but were also more critical and less warm and affectionate with their children.[44]

In *How to Raise an Adult*, author Julie Lythcott-Haims cites a talk by Dr. Madeline Levine, who said there are three ways we are overparenting (overprotecting and overcontrolling) and "unwittingly causing psychological harm: 1. when we do for our kids what they can *already* do for themselves; 2. when we do for our kids what they can *almost* do for themselves; and 3. when our parenting behavior is motivated by our own ego."[45]

It's not too late, though, and that's what the rest of the book is about. We can change the course of things for your daughter now. However, for her to learn to problem-solve, you're going to have to stop solving her problems. She's going to have to learn to do the scary thing. It's going to need to be a team effort. And you, as the parent, are going to have to go first.

A new type of treatment has emerged at Yale called SPACE. It stands for Supportive Parenting for Anxious Childhood Emotions.

In it, the only ones who get the therapy are the parents themselves. Parents learn to recognize ways they accommodate their children's anxiety. They're taught to express confidence in their children and to face their fears and deal with uncomfortable feelings. And then, the parents are taught how to gradually help their children do the scary thing.[46]

Children who have anxiety feel like they're "less than" other kids. They feel less capable, less durable, less hopeful, less able, less confident. They have less trust in others, less trust in their own intuition. They feel like they have less control over their environment and less control over their own emotions. They feel less than. And out of that less than, worry becomes as natural to them as breathing.

Children who worry seek comfort and certainty. They don't feel much of either, in their less than-ness. And so they look to you. You are their safe place. They hide behind you if given the chance. They'll let you answer the "what if" questions and solve the problems and fight the monsters for them. But this Worry Monster is one that she has to fight herself. And you might have to fight your own right alongside her. It is terrifying, at times. You love this little girl like crazy, and, of course, you want to protect her. You want to take care of her. And, at times, everything inside of you is going to want to rescue her.

You're probably ready for me to throw my studies out the window at this point. But another cited in *The Self-Driven Child* reports that "other than showing your child love and affection, managing your own stress is the best thing you can do to be an effective parent."[47] I would add, not just an effective parent but an empowering parent. As you manage your own stress, you model for her that she can do the same. You teach her that she is capable, that she's braver and stronger and smarter than she knows. When you give her opportunities to solve her own problems, to develop resourcefulness, to do the scary thing, you teach her that she's so much more. That becomes your parenting style. And it is reflective of not only what you believe about her, but what God does too. He's got her. There is always hope. And help is on the way.

Key Points to Remember

- Your daughter worries because she cares. Things matter to her, which can make life hard. It's hard for her to know how to turn that care off.
- Anxiety is the primary mental health problem facing children today.
- Girls are more likely to have anxiety but are brought in less for treatment because their anxiety is missed or misinterpreted.
- Girls feel an inordinate amount of pressure from society, from the culture around them, from social media, from their own expectations of themselves, and sometimes from our expectations of them. This pressure often translates to anxiety.
- We've shortened the childhood of girls by a year and a half.
- Technology and social media add to the pressure girls face today and, according to a wide variety of research, contribute significantly to their anxiety. They need us to help them gradually learn responsible technology use.
- We want to give girls coping skills to handle the pressure as well as help them value the effort more than the outcome.
- Because girls want to please and don't yet understand their own feelings of anxiety, their worries can be misinterpreted. Their outsides often don't match their insides.
- Girls lean toward exploding and taking their worries out on others or imploding and taking those worries out on themselves.
- Fifteen to 20 percent of children are born with temperaments that predispose them to worry. Gifted children are among those predisposed to worry, as are children who have an inherent negativity bias.

- We want to help girls work through hurt and trauma in healthy ways by being safe places for them and getting them the help they need to prevent trauma from transforming into anxiety.
- A child is seven times more likely to develop an anxiety disorder when they have a parent who suffers from anxiety.
- Genetics only determine 30–40 percent of anxiety in kids—the rest is determined by temperament, life experiences, parental modeling, and parenting styles.

Understanding Yourself and Your Daughter Better

What do you believe has contributed to your daughter's worries?

Why do you think anxiety is an epidemic among children today? Why do you think girls might feel more anxiety, but their anxiety is recognized less?

What kind of pressure is your daughter under?

What kinds of expectations do you put on her, without meaning to? What kinds of expectations does she put on herself?

How do technology and social media affect your daughter?

What could you be doing now to help her learn responsible technology use?

What is your daughter like when she's worried? Is she more of an exploder or an imploder? What about you?

How have you seen your daughter's temperament contribute to her worries?

Are there life experiences you believe have contributed to your daughter's worry? In her life or your family's? How has she processed those experiences?

What has been your family history, in terms of anxiety? What about your own journey?

How do you model your own strategies for handling worry? How do you talk about your worries?

How would you describe your parenting style? Do you think there are ways your parenting style might be contributing to her worries without you realizing it?

What are you doing for her today that she could be doing for herself?

3. How Will This Help?

I really wish we were sitting together in my counseling office, at this point. I wish I could lean toward you and smile. I wish we could laugh a little about how the pressure on parents might rival what she feels. At least she gets recess or P.E.

So far, we've been walking through some heavy things. And the worst is over—almost. More than two and a half decades of counseling girls has given me visible proof that anxiety is at epidemic levels. But in the past three years in particular, I've observed something else: Anxiety has become a trend.

The Problem of Perspective

Over the years, I've known a lot of girls who have worn ankle braces. I'm quite sure each and every brace wasn't truly needed for a physical injury. It's like little kids and Band-Aids. They want people to know they got a boo-boo and that it hurt a bit, so they wear a Band-Aid. Or several. As they get older, they might take a spill from their bike and "need" an ACE bandage around their elbow. Then they enter middle school, they start to play competitive sports, and you spend a lot of time at Walgreens, quickly learning that every injury doesn't necessitate a trip to the doctor. Braces certainly help a great deal, especially with walking around at school. Orthopedic boots help even more. And now they've even got that cool sports injury tape at CVS. (Hello, marketers who must know some of these children and brilliantly made the tape in neon colors!) If I'm describing your daughter, you know exactly what I'm talking about.

The use of Band-Aids and braces and orthopedic boots is frequently genuine, but as I said, they can also be outward signs of inward hurt. They can signal that she feels unsure or unsteady, like she's not quite confident in her place in the world. Or maybe she's worried or anxious but doesn't have the words to say so. Whatever is going on inside, these girls in braces are trying to express that they're needing more. I wouldn't necessarily call it attention seeking, although it could be. They want to be seen and known and loved. And what I've observed in these girls, it's a little easier to be seen when you have a piece of neon tape wrapped around your shoulder.

These girls might also be struggling with their perspective. In our book *Are My Kids on Track?* we suggest a 1 to 10 scale for evaluating one's perspective. I jokingly call it a drama-mometer, because I work with so many girls. As adults, we know that daily life is usually in the 2 to 7 range. Extremes are rare. But there are girls (and boys) for whom everything that happens is a 10, or even 10-plus! Her teacher is the "meanest in the world"; it was the "worst day ever"; or she announces, "I was so freaked out I almost lost my mind!" These girls struggle with the developmental milestone of perspective.

Briefly, here's how the drama-mometer can help your girl. When your daughter is in a calmer moment, talk about the scale (she doesn't need to know we call it a drama-mometer; we can keep that between us). Help her imagine what a 10 on the perspective scale truly is, and also a 7, and maybe a 3. Then, when she gets in the car and says something extreme, like her friends "hate me and never want to talk to me again!" respond first with empathy. Listen, and then refer to the scale. "That sounds like a really hard day. What number do you think it was on your scale?"

The perspective struggle is trickier today than it used to be. When I was growing up, the worst thing you could say to your parents on a 10 kind of day was "I want to run away from home!" I have not heard a child talk about running away from home in years. Now they say, "I want to kill myself." And kids are not just saying it—they're attempting it. In the last ten years, the rate of hospital admissions for suicidal children and adolescents has almost tripled, according to doctor and reporter Perri Klass. "And the rate of increase was highest among adolescent girls," she says.[1]

Almost daily I see girls who have diagnosed themselves with depression and/or anxiety-related issues such as panic attacks, post-traumatic stress disorder (PTSD), and obsessive-compulsive disorder (OCD). This past year alone I have noticed that when I simply ask new clients, "So what brought you to Daystar?" they often list off the criteria for major depressive disorder or generalized anxiety disorder, as if they memorized them from the internet.

A good number of these girls are genuinely struggling. As I have said, I've never seen so many children suffer from debilitating anxiety or depression. I've also never had to hospitalize as many girls out of concern they might try to take their own lives. And there will also be kids who need an outward sign of inward hurt or want big words to describe the big feelings inside of them.

One girl I was counseling, a high schooler, started describing to me the symptoms of depression. Soon she was using the word itself, and she asked me if I thought she was depressed. I didn't want to jump on the diagnosis train with her if she wasn't clinically depressed, so I sidestepped the question for a time and just kept listening. Next, she started saying things like, "My friend Allison is taking medicine, and it seems like it's really helping her."

Here was my concern. I do believe she had some of what I consider low-grade depression. But I also don't believe in diagnosing kids, unless they really need a diagnosis. Children, particularly teenagers, are looking for ways to define themselves. And I don't want anxiety or depression or eating disorders or another type of struggle to become their identity. But as is always the case, context helps this girl's story make more sense. We'll call her Gracie.

Gracie is a great friend. She listens well, and she's honestly one of the most encouraging freshmen in high school I know. She wants everyone she meets to feel loved. She has walked with several friends through their own crises—times of depression and even suicide attempts. Last fall, she started to struggle herself. I think it was honestly just carrying that much weight for that long, bless her heart. So, she started to have a hard time, and I think none of her friends was listening to her, at least not with the compassion and consistency with which she had been listening to them. So Gracie needed big words and something potentially really wrong to get friends and others to turn their attention toward her (which is a great illustration of why I'm concerned about the lack of perspective among girls today).

Gracie's mom was brilliant. I brought her up to my office because I wanted her to hear from Gracie herself how hard things felt. Her mom turned toward Gracie on the couch, put her hand on her shoulder, and listened to her with such kindness and compassion. With her mom, Gracie used the word *depression* and even suggested that she thought she needed medication. Gracie's wise mom responded like this: "Gracie, I'm so sad things have been so tough lately. I hate it for you. I'm with you in it. I hear you that you feel alone and things don't seem to be getting better. I know your friends haven't been there for you in the way you'd hoped. But you're not alone. I'm here. And I get that you feel really deep sadness right now. It is *deep sadness*. I see it. I want to listen and want you to feel like you can talk to me about it anytime. But I also don't want your deep sadness to make you feel like you're depressed. I watched you laugh with Alexis yesterday. You really needed to laugh. And I know that you had a pretty good time on our trip to the mountains this summer. When you're clinically depressed, you don't have those moments when things feel better. The deep sadness doesn't come and go in that way. I want to listen to your sadness. I want you to know I believe it's real. And hard.

But I also don't want you to decide that something is harder than it has to be. And I never want you to give up hope."

I wish I had a video of Gracie's mom saying those words, because I would replay it to girls in my office daily. She has done a lot of her own work in counseling, and they need to soak in her main message: *Your pain is important, but you don't have to make it bigger than it is just for me to hear you or to make it valid.*

I've had girls tell me that no one will truly listen to them unless they have anxiety or depression or they are cutting themselves. Let's listen to them and validate their feelings. And let's help them find appropriate words to describe their big emotions. Let's use the drama-mometer scale to show them that their feelings matter, but also to give them the context of perspective. And while we're at it, let's use appropriate words to describe our own feelings. How often do we throw around extreme words when we're describing ourselves or others? ("I had a panic attack when I couldn't find my phone!")

A lack of perspective or knowledge is another danger in the big-words-to-describe-big-feelings phenomenon. We believe our girl when she says she was bullied (a "big" word) at school, when really a close friend simply chose someone else to play with on that particular day. In another case, a mom recently told me her daughter had the worst year of her life. She went on to describe what I would consider some pretty normal middle school drama and then said, "And today was the worst of all. She even stepped in dog poop!"

Dog poop stinks, we would all agree. But there are things that "stink" a lot worse and have the power to actually ruin a day. Dog poop is not even a 3 on the drama-mometer scale. I'd put it at less than 1, maybe point-4.

Don't hop on the 10 side of the scale with her. Be aware that there is always more to a story. There's another side. And she may be using big words just to get your attention.

Because girls with anxiety overestimate threats or problems and underestimate themselves, you can see how a lack of perspective can make both sides of that equation worse. We want to keep empowering her. We want to help her see hard situations as learning opportunities. We want to validate her feelings and, at the same time, help her feel that she's braver and stronger and smarter than anything life can throw at her.

What Doesn't Work

Here's what we've established thus far: Your daughter is growing up in an age of anxiety. It's in the words girls use today, it has infiltrated their culture, it's a part of the pressure they feel to perform in school. And sports. And the arts. It's a part of the busyness of their lives, between practices and lessons and social lives . . . not to mention social media. It may even be in their genes. Girls want to do well, be liked, live up to their own expectations and yours, and look pretty at the same time. And they don't want to fail or hurt anyone's feelings. It's a lot. And so they worry even more.

The problem, as you likely know, is that efforts to control worry don't work. Have you ever tried to just stop worrying? It's the same as trying not to think about something.

Years ago I was talking with a friend who is a professional recording artist, and she told me her doctor said one of the worst things she could do for her singing voice was to clear her throat. Know what I immediately felt like I had to do? Clear my throat. (Is your throat tickling a little right now too?)

This is an actual scientific phenomenon. Fyodor Dostoyevsky, whom you may remember from his literary classic *The Brothers Karamazov*, first talked about it in his essay "Winter Notes on Summer Impressions":

> Try to pose for yourself this task: not to think of a polar bear, and you will see that the cursed thing will come to mind every minute.[2]

Sounds a little like the intrusive thoughts we talked about early in this book, doesn't it? In 1987, a social psychologist and professor at Harvard, Daniel Wegner, proved that theory. He found the more we try to suppress a thought, the more the thought comes to life.[3]

You might have tried to turn off troubling thoughts yourself in times past. I'm guessing it didn't work, right? But somehow, you still tell your daughter to stop thinking about throwing up. Or stop worrying about a test. Or stop thinking something bad will happen to you on your trip. It doesn't help. She may stop talking about it out of a desire to please you, but she doesn't stop thinking about it. And that, honestly, makes things even worse, because then we don't know what's happening in her mind and heart. We want to equip her with ways to manage her worry, rather than just go underground with it.

Many parents of girls who wrestle with worry come into my offices frustrated.

"We can't reason with her."

"We've told her that everything will be fine, but she doesn't believe us."

"When she gets really upset, there's no way to talk her out of it."

"When she starts to worry, it's like she loses control. Her thoughts just get less and less rational, and her emotions get more and more out of control. Then, we're in a full-scale meltdown, and everyone is yelling."

Logic doesn't work. Trying to reason with her doesn't work. Punishment doesn't even work. The more she tries not to worry, the more she worries. She's frustrated, and you become frustrated right alongside her. Or even at her. And that doesn't work either.

I talk to parents every day who feel like they're being held hostage by their daughter's anxiety. They spend great amounts of time and go to great lengths to avoid the things that make her worry. They answer the what-if questions ad nauseum. They reassure, coax, accommodate. In fact, escape and avoidance are two of the most common ways kids and the adults who love them try to control anxiety, according to the authors of *The Anxiety and Worry Workbook*.[4] Both only make the Worry Monster stronger. Neither work, at least not for very long.

The anxiety continues to control your daughter, instead of her learning to control it. You're exhausted and frustrated, as is the rest of your family. As one mom said to me, "Anxiety isn't just a problem for my daughter. At this point, it's a problem for our entire family."

So we've established the bad news. We've talked about what doesn't work. Now let's get to the good news—what fills the rest of the book: what *does* work and how you can help your girl be the boss of that bossy Worry Monster.

Therapy: A Cure for Anxiety?

When it comes to therapy, you may have heard of CBT, DBT, EFT, or EMDR. They're all acronyms describing some of the most prevalent approaches or types of therapy today. As with so many things, types of counseling wax and wane in popularity. But all of these approaches, as well as many others, have situations and contexts in which they're particularly useful and therapeutic.

Bridget Flynn Walker, a clinical psychologist and author, asserts that CBT (cognitive behavioral therapy) is the most researched therapy and has the most evidence-based results.[5] With CBT, its name reflects the premise: The way we think influences how we feel and, therefore, how we behave. So, if we change the way we think, it changes not only how we feel but also the way we act.

CBT can be helpful for people of all ages, including young children. I started working with Abbye when she was nine years old. Right away I could tell she was extremely bright. From her parents, I learned there was a history of anxiety in the family, including in Abbye's mom, who had battled it, to some degree, most of her life. Abbye had experienced worried thoughts and anxious behavior for years before I met her, but her parents hadn't connected the dots until they brought her in to see me. Abbye tried to counter her worries by trying hard at everything she did and trying to please her parents. By the time she came in to see me, though, her anxiety had quietly entrenched itself in her thinking, feelings, and behavior.

As a brief aside, experts don't agree on the typical onset age of anxiety. For years, I had read and experienced in my practice that anxiety could begin around the age of eight. Some research says the age is eleven, and I definitely see an uptick in anxiety and its symptoms in girls at that age, which I think has a great deal to do with entering puberty. But the most recent data I found reports that the average age of onset is six.[6]

Initially, Abbye came to my office for separation anxiety. She and I met for several months, during which we worked on understanding her worries and learning CBT tools to fight that Worry Monster. She worked on breathing, relaxation, and grounding techniques, all of which I'll explain in the next section. She learned how her worries play tricks on her and what she could do to boss back those worries. When she ended counseling, she was feeling stronger and in control of her worries, rather than her worries controlling her. I didn't see Abbye for two years.

Then Abbye's parents brought her back to see me. Her fears had shifted. The family had an upcoming trip, and she had suddenly developed a fear of flying. I can't say I was surprised. Anxiety can be a little like a bad penny—it can keep coming back to you. As we discussed in chapter 1, anxiety is closely tied to a child's development. What triggers your girl's worries, or the things her looping thoughts focus on, will evolve as she gets older. Our goal is for her to learn to manage her anxiety, rather than find a magical cure. I frequently tell parents of anxious girls at our first meeting the same thing I told Abbye's parents: "Your daughter may deal with some degree of anxiety for her entire life. She's smart. She's conscientious. And she cares. She's not going to change the fact that things matter deeply to her. Therefore, this is going to circle back around with different themes potentially forever. But she can learn the tools to fight it. And that fight will get easier every time it comes back."

The fact that Abbye's anxiety returned didn't mean that counseling didn't "take" the first time. With the tools she learned then, she knew how to handle it better when it came back. She knew the Worry Monster's tricks, recognized them, and went to work fighting them with the help of her parents and with me. She's actually the one who requested to see me again, asking, "Mom, I think my worries are getting worse again. Can we go see Sissy?"

This time, we focused Abbye's tools on a fear of flying. I suggested she imagine herself the morning of the flight and then taking off and landing, all while practicing relaxation techniques. We talked about her worst fears, and then learned statistics about the safety of planes. We came up with things she could do to refocus if she became anxious, such as math problems (counting backward from one hundred by sevens, for example) or color exercises (finding everything in her view that was a certain color). She changed her thinking, which influenced her feelings and, therefore, changed her behavior.

I haven't seen Abbye for almost a year. She's been successfully traveling with her parents since that time. My guess is that I'll see Abbye again, though. Her worry will be back, although I think it will come back to an even lesser degree the next time. And she'll know how to handle it more quickly. Or maybe she'll remember the tools without me. The tools she learned and that we will talk about in this book find their origins in cognitive behavioral therapy, and they're tools that can be directed toward any type of anxiety . . . as many times as it returns.

. . . .

When I was doing research for this book, I read twenty-three books on the subject. Every one of them talked about how we all live with some degree of anxiety. We all have a Worry Monster, whether he's big or small. Your daughter's brain is most malleable during childhood. She's got the best chances now to learn and remember tools to fight her Worry Monster. How much do you wish you had learned these kinds of tools when you were eight or ten or eleven years of age? Your worry would still be there at times, but you'd have had more practice and more time to build up confidence in your own strength.

Let me say one last time before we move on: I don't believe any of us is ever "cured" from anxiety, because of the way anxiety is tied to our temperaments and our giftedness. Abbye will likely always worry at least a little, because she is bright and conscientious, just like I'm sure your daughter is. It's the flip side of the coin of her giftedness. Courage with fear is wisdom; courage without fear is destructiveness. Abbye has a lot of wisdom that comes with her fear. And she's found a lot of courage. We're going to help your daughter do the same.

Where We're Headed

We'll be learning about many CBT tools in this book. You'll have exercises you can do with your daughter and on your own that will help change her and your thinking and, therefore, your feelings and behaviors. But we'll also talk about what might be going on underneath your daughter's anxiety. I have noticed over the years that a child who is prone to worry often worries at key moments.

The firstborn daughter who has noticed her parents seem to be fighting more has a surge in her fear of monsters. Her parents, however, didn't know that she had overheard the arguments or seen the angry glances across the table.

Another little girl whose brother was diagnosed with cancer suddenly develops a lot of worries about her grades. Her parents don't pressure her to make good grades. She's always done well on her own. But her grades are something she can control, and the cancer that's affecting her brother isn't.

The teenager who has randomly developed a fear of going out in public was chastised by a teacher in front of her peers the first time she was in a school play, which also happened to be when she stopped wanting to leave her house.

It's not just age or hormones that dictate when a child will struggle with worries the most. It's also deeper issues of her heart. And, of course, it has to do with her faith too. Our worries are tied to the physical, mental, emotional, and spiritual parts of who we are. They sometimes originate in one of those places, but the Worry Monster will try to work his wily ways in all areas of her life.

Worries typically show up first in the body, revving up her nervous system so much that she can't fight the Worry Monster. The fight-or-flight region of her brain takes over, and logic and reason go out the window. She can't talk herself out of her worries, and neither can you. But if we can equip her with some tools to calm her body back down, she'll be able to think more clearly to fight him in the very thoughts he comes after next.

The next part of your daughter—her thinking—is where, as CBT theory asserts, her worries really take hold. The Worry Monster has some tried-and-true tricks to make her think a problem is too big, or she's too small to handle it. We'll be going after several of those tricks specifically, with ways she can arm herself against them. She's going to discover a voice that is louder and stronger than the chaotic noise of her worries. We're going to teach her to shut that Worry Monster down at every turn.

Next, he tries to sink his claws down deep into her heart. He comes after her when she's most vulnerable and tries to tell her she's not capable. She needs to hide. And she needs you to protect her. We want to remind her of who God has made her to be and see her step into the courage that is inside of her. Then you're going to help her come up with a plan to move toward the very things she's afraid of and, therefore, find more courage than she even thought was possible.

And finally, we're going to arm her with truth so that when the Worry Monster comes back with his whac-a-mole ways, she'll have an unshakable foundation from which to fight him. Her faith can be her strongest and steadiest tool. God wants her to have peace and strength and hope in Him. We want to help her find her way to that kind of faith.

Along the way, we'll talk about the Worry Monster's most common tricks and the tools you and your girl can use to fight him. As you read the chapters ahead, there will be many examples of different fears. It doesn't matter what the specifics of her fears are right now. They shift over time and throughout her development. Her level of worry will wax and wane. But the tools you will learn work with any fear. Fighting the Worry Monster is likely going to be the hardest battle she's ever fought. Because she'll be the one doing the bulk of the fighting, it may be one of your hardest battles as well.

A Few Things to Keep in Mind

Let's go back to my little yellow office at Daystar. We're sitting across from each other at the end of our first session. You're on the couch. I'm in my chair. My little dog, Lucy, is sleeping in the corner, ready to have more time with your daughter. Your daughter is downstairs waiting to get this Worry Monster battle started. She's ready for things to be different. And so are you. You both understand now more of what's happening with her worries. Here's where the real help begins. As we pull her into the process, these are the three things I most want you to remember.

1. The work is hers, not yours. Did you notice how much we talked about her doing different things in the last section? Arming her, teaching her, equipping her? There are things you need to learn and do, but the worry-fighting work is ultimately hers. You can't fight this battle for her, as much as you'd like to. She's going to have to do the scary thing, and you're going to have to allow her. You can stand beside her and cheer her on every step of the way. Yes, therapy is more effective when parents are involved. But she still has to do the work. It is only when she does the work herself that she experiences the reward. In fact, the more worried she is, the more confidence she gets when she accomplishes the scary task. You don't want to take away that self-esteem or hard-won courage by fighting the battle for her, or even allowing her to skip it.

2. Practice makes progress.[7] This is one of David's favorite statements in *Are My Kids on Track?*, and one of mine, too, as we enter this battle with worry. This process is going to be a three-steps-forward, two-steps-back kind of situation. Fighting worries is hard work, in a trudging sort of way. The Worry Monster hides in the stickiest, sludgiest places of her mind and heart, and so she's going to have to be tenacious in the fight. She'll need your encouragement to practice, and practice daily. She'll also need you to rejoice in any forward movement. It's the process, not the outcome. And any step in the fight is a step toward her finding her courage.

3. She's braver than she believes, stronger than she seems, and smarter than she thinks. She is also braver than you might believe, stronger than you might think she seems, and smarter than anyone knows (except for God, that is). These statements are variations of something Christopher Robin said to Winnie-the-Pooh. And interestingly, the quote really begins with, "If ever there is a tomorrow when we're not together."[8] It seems fitting, because separation anxiety is often the place where a girl's worries start. Pooh and A. A. Milne knew. . . .

The original title of the girls' activity book was *Braver, Stronger, Smarter, and More Loved Than You Know*. But we changed it in the editing process because we didn't want girls to believe their love was tied in any way to their anxiety. Even so, love is the bottom line. That love is why and how this book is going to help. Because underneath all of the tools we're going to learn and all of the practice she's going to do, the main purpose is to remind her of how deeply she is loved by a God who sees her, knows her, and understands her and every bit of her worries. He created her as the brave, strong, and smart girl that she is right now. In fact, that's one of the first things I tell her in her book: "This book is not meant to make you braver and stronger and smarter than you are, because you are every one of those things already. It's just meant to open your eyes to the bravery, strength, and smarts that God placed deep inside of you."

It's all there. She needs you to remember that for you and for her. She can do this. And so can you. You're both loved more than you know by a God who has given her all that she needs to fight the Worry Monster. And you will always be one of her best tools.

Key Points to Remember

- Anxiety is not just an epidemic. It's also a trend among kids today.
- Girls struggle at times with the milestone of perspective, needing big words to describe big emotions.
- The rate of hospitalization for children and teens with suicidal ideation or who have attempted suicide has almost tripled in the past ten years. The rates among girls has shown the greatest increase.
- Children are looking for ways to define themselves, and we don't want them to define themselves by their struggles.
- A lack of perspective makes her feel that the problem is bigger and she is smaller. She needs your help.
- Trying to stop worrying doesn't work any more than you can stop thinking about a polar bear. (See?)
- Escape and avoidance are the two strategies most often used by girls and their parents to control anxiety. Neither strategy helps the problem.
- CBT is the most research-driven therapeutic approach to anxiety. It's based on the idea that the way we think affects the way we feel, which affects the way we behave.
- Anxiety comes back with different themes across her development. With help, girls (and their parents) learn how to lessen its power each time.

- Her worries impact her physically, mentally, emotionally, and spiritually. In this book, we're going to fight the Worry Monster on all levels. We'll learn his tricks, give her tools, and arm her with truth to discover the brave, strong, smart girl God has made her to be.

Understanding Yourself and Your Daughter Better

How is your daughter's sense of perspective? How has she learned or not learned this milestone?

How is your daughter trying to define herself today?

How could you help her find more of a sense of perspective?

How have you tried to get your daughter to stop worrying in the past? What has worked and what hasn't? What about with your own worries?

What is an example you can think of where the way you think has influenced the way you feel and, therefore, the way you behave? What is an example of this in your daughter?

Think about a timeline for your daughter's worries. How have they evolved and with what major life events have they coincided?

What are your hopes for your daughter as you move forward with this journey?

What do you want her to know about herself?

What do you believe you can do to help? What would you like to change about how you help her fight her worries?

What do you want to remember as you go forward?

HELP

4. Help for Her Body

In the past two weeks I've had fourteen first-time appointments with girls and their families. Every single family came in with a daughter somewhere on the worry continuum. The worry had different origins and different expressions, but the Worry Monster is hijacking the body, mind, and heart of each of those girls. Fourteen out of fourteen. And their parents are desperate for help.

I find myself being firmer with parents than I used to be about helping their children overcome anxiety. I'm not looking to feed any mom guilt or dad guilt you might feel. It's not your fault your daughter is struggling. Even if you have unknowingly done things that enable the worry, the important thing to focus on is growing your coping skills right alongside hers. Remember: We all worry to some degree. But there is a physical component to anxiety that is especially hard on children, so she needs your help. You are instrumental in turning the worry tide for her.

I wholeheartedly agree with this statement by the authors of *Parent-Led CBT for Child Anxiety*: "Parents are the most important agent for change that we [therapists] can access in helping children to overcome difficulties with anxiety."[1]

The Worry Monster's Tricks for Her

Several years ago, I was on a bike ride with my dear friend Melissa Trevathan, who founded Daystar Counseling. We were riding through flat Kentucky farmland when we spotted a storm several miles away but starting to blow in. Concerned, we picked up our pace. We could see lightning strikes in the distance, and although we felt pretty safe, we sped up and pedaled as fast as we could. Melissa was probably fifty yards in front of me when a lightning bolt literally hit the ground between us. I immediately threw my bike down and started running for a nearby cornfield. *A cornfield? Like that was going to protect me?* Regardless, there was no part of me that stopped, looked around for the nearest shelter, rode my bike to the shoulder, and put the kickstand down. No, I left my bike in the middle of the road and hightailed it to a cornfield. I wasn't thinking. I was reacting to the fear shooting through me like an electric current. My reaction was a survival instinct.

In His wisdom, God gave us an emergency response system: a series of actions our brains and bodies make to keep us or others alive in an emergency. You have likely experienced this many times as a parent. When your girl was a toddler, did she ever fall down, say, while running down the driveway? I'm guessing you sprang toward her faster than you ever imagined possible. There is no end to dramatic stories of moms and dads having superhuman strength in the midst of danger.

These survival skills kick in without us thinking. Your body locks into a system of responses dictated by your nervous system. It happens within seconds. Did you notice which system this involves? Yep, those good old nervous nerves.

Here's an overview of what happens: The autonomic nervous system determines certain automatic functions in our body. It has two primary branches: the sympathetic nervous system (fight-or-flight) and the parasympathetic nervous system (rest and digest). The sympathetic nervous system is what takes over when we're afraid.

"Fear kicks your fight-or-flight response into overdrive," says a *Right as Rain* article citing psychologist Daniel Evans. "Your adrenal glands secrete adrenaline. Blood flow decreases to your brain's frontal lobe, which is responsible for logical thinking and planning, and the deeper, more animalistic parts of your brain—including the amygdala—take over."[2] Then every part of your body works together for one purpose: survival. Your heart and breathing rate go up; your blood pressure increases. God even designed your pupils to dilate so you could see the danger more clearly. Your blood shifts more toward your larger muscles, so that you are tensed and ready, with cold, clammy hands and perspiration to prove it.[3] In other words, God made our bodies so that we could run faster into cornfields to escape lightning bolts. Your stomach jumps on board with the alarm by decreasing your digestive activity so that you have all the energy you need to fight or flee. Blood even leaves your skin so that you won't bleed as much if you're injured.

We truly are fearfully and wonderfully made. But sometimes our brains operate on false alarms.

An Amygdala Under Siege

The amygdala is notorious for false alarms, especially in the 15 to 20 percent of individuals who have a hyperreactive amygdala to begin with. This means **your daughter is not thinking clearly when she's anxious. In fact, the more anxious she gets, the less clearly she thinks.** The blood flow shifts away from her prefrontal cortex—the part of the brain where she plans, thinks rationally, and manages her emotions—and shifts to her amygdala, the fight-or-flight region of her brain. The amygdala, in essence, hijacks her brain in those moments. So no amount of logic on your part is loud enough to drown out the wail of her amygdala until we teach her to slow her sympathetic nervous system back down. (More on this later in the chapter in the "Tools for Her" section.)

The funny thing is, while I've been working on this chapter, Melissa, David, and I have been speaking at an out-of-town event in Florida. The first night, after writing the previous paragraph, I was awakened by a chirping sound in my hotel room. Every two minutes. Chirp . . . chirp . . . chirp. It took a bit, but I realized the battery in the smoke alarm needed to be replaced. Guess what it was causing? A false alarm—a false alarm that repeated itself over and over and over. You know how it is to be awakened in the middle of the night. I decided that a sound machine app on my phone was a better decision than calling maintenance, knowing I'd really never be able to fall back asleep if they came in my room and turned on all of the lights. So, I drifted on and off to sleep with the chirp in the background. The next morning, I called the front desk immediately.

Night two, exhausted after speaking for six hours that day, I was more than thrilled at the silence in my room. I fell asleep early after watching a show on my iPad, knowing I had an early flight home the next morning. And then at one in the morning it started. Chirp. CHIRP. CHIRP! I have no idea what happened, but the false alarm was back on, and I thought I might lose my mind. I literally slept on top of my phone with the noise machine app going all night. You would have thought I was in a tent in the rain forest by the sounds coming from my bed. The chirp was relentless and infuriating. I couldn't think about anything but the noise. I felt like a crazy person all night long and was exhausted in the aftermath . . . which is much the way your daughter feels when her amygdala hijacks her brain.

A Body Tensed for Tension

When her amygdala takes over, your daughter's body is poised to respond. Every portion of her sympathetic nervous system goes into overdrive: her stomach, her head, her hands, her thoughts, even her vision. Just this week I had a high school freshman tell me about a panic attack during a math test where the numbers were "swimming" in front of her.

When worry and anxiety hit, your daughter will likely feel light-headed and dizzy. She may become teary and complain of a headache.

Her chest may feel tight and her heart may pound. She may shake and sweat. She may breathe faster than normal and feel like she can't get enough air—all descriptors of a panic attack. In addition, she may feel nauseated, her stomach may hurt, and she may get diarrhea and even vomit. It sounds awful, doesn't it? And these symptoms can flare up in less than half a second in response to a triggering event or thought.[4]

In the long run, girls can end up panicking over panic. Their experience with fear will be so terrible that they never want to feel that kind of misery again.

A teenager I counseled recently had anxiety that spiked during school, resulting in a mild panic attack. She wears a smart watch and noticed that her heart rate became elevated during the episode. She now checks her watch in school incessantly, worried that her heart rate will spike again. She is worrying about the worry and its effect on her body. With anxiety, children (and adults) often become more fearful about the fear itself than the event that triggered the fear to begin with, primarily because of the havoc that fear wreaks on their entire body.

Too many children (and their parents) never realize that worry is the monster attacking their bodies. I have seen several girls over the years who blame general but persistent stomach problems for everything that ails them . . . and don't really want to be told anything different. These tend to be the strong, perfectionistic, can't-stand-to-be-vulnerable girls, and having an anxious stomach would make them appear weak, they think. Others have appointment after appointment with pediatricians, finally to hear that there is no medical cause for their headaches. Then they end up in my office.

Let me say, however, that even if a girl's physical symptoms don't have a medical basis, her pain is real. She's not faking. Her body really does register the effects of her worries, even if she doesn't yet understand what's happening. She'll need the pediatrician and you to help her connect the dots and get the help she needs before those dots expand.

The Long-Term Impact

The amygdala is efficient. When it decides there's cause for alarm, it sounds that alarm loudly and persistently, just like that malfunctioning smoke alarm in my hotel room. Worry is the most common cause for an amygdala's false alarm. Chronic worry makes the alarm not only more faulty, but much harder to turn off.

Chronic stress actually enlarges the amygdala, creating even more vulnerability to fear, anxiety, and anger. Robert Sapolsky, Stanford University professor and stress expert, says, "Chronic stress creates a hyper-reactive, hysterical amygdala."[5] *Hysterical* seems to be a particularly fitting word. The amygdala enlarges and develops what is referred to as a hair-trigger response.

In one of our favorite books at Daystar, *The Yes Brain*, Daniel Siegel and Tina Payne Bryson write how the brain is essentially rewired during worry.

> The actual physical architecture of the brain adapts to new information, reorganizing itself and creating neural pathways based on what a person sees, hears, touches, thinks about, practices, and so on. . . . Where attention goes, neurons fire. And where neurons fire, they wire, or join together.[6]

In other words, brains that worry chronically become wired to worry even more.

For teenagers, their brains are already on overload. This means stress impacts the adolescent brain even more significantly. In their book *The Self-Driven Child*, William Stixrud and Ned Johnson explain that "animal studies have found that after a prolonged period of stress, the adult brain will tend to bounce back within ten days, while the adolescent brain takes about three weeks."[7]

Worry affects your daughter's brain significantly. But it affects yours too. Yes, the Worry Monster has a specific set of tricks to impact you and your ability to parent your worried child.

The Worry Monster's Tricks for You

Logic and Reason

If there is one primary emotion I hear from parents of girls who worry, it's frustration.

"I try to tell her how unreasonable she's being, but she won't listen."

"There's no talking to her when she gets like this!"

Almost every parent says some version of the same sentence. Care to guess my first response? I educate the parents on the false alarm of the amygdala. I talk about how their daughter's brain becomes flooded with adrenaline and dopamine, which make it impossible for her to think clearly. She's not logical. She's literally incapable of reason when her sympathetic nervous system kicks into survival gear. Until she can calm down, she is unable to talk herself out of the worries. And so are you.

What should happen next? Help her take deep breaths. Put your arm around her. Try to soothe her. Tell her, "Honey, everything is fine. You don't need to worry. I'm not going to let anything bad happen to you." Coax her out of the chaos of her emotions.

Emotion and Escalation

When my dog, Lucy, was a puppy, we went to puppy school. My lasting memory is the instructor scolding me—yes, me—not my dog. We were practicing separation, and I was supposed to leave Lucy in a spot and then return. But when I put Lucy in a sit position and told her to stay, she whined. That's when my dog parenting skills went out the window. "Lucy, you're okay. Don't worry. I'll be back soon," I said in what I thought was a comforting voice. (Lucy, of course, had no idea what I was saying.) According to the dog trainer, my attempts to comfort Lucy sounded like a whine in her language, and she would actually become more anxious, thinking there was even more wrong than she thought. Hmmm . . .

Speaking of dogs, when Lucy and I came into view of a seven-year-old girl at Daystar recently, the girl started screaming and jumped onto the back of the couch behind her mom. Her mom wrapped her arms around her, pulled her into her chest, and said, "Oh, honey. I'm so sorry. That dog is not going to get you." And then she glared at me and said sternly, "She's very afraid of dogs." Have I mentioned that Lucy is a whopping eight pounds? And have I also mentioned that it's *her* office?

Yes, I might have been a little irritated by the show of emotion from both of them. But I was also disappointed for that young girl. Her mom, in her attempts to comfort her daughter, communicated to her that there was a reason to be comforted. She needed rescuing. I wished the mom had said, "Honey, you're okay. Take a few breaths." Maybe then she could have stood up, kissed her daughter on the head, and added something like, "Oh, what a cute dog. May I pet her?" She could have talked to her daughter about how small Lucy was, or how sweet, or she wouldn't even have had to say a word. But, regardless, in any of those statements, she would have been communicating that there was nothing to be afraid of.

"Anxiety is a method of seeking two experiences: *certainty* and *comfort*. The problem is that it wants these two outcomes *immediately* and *continually*," according to Reid Wilson and Lynn Lyons, the authors of *Anxious Kids, Anxious Parents*.[8] To give children the certainty and comfort they're seeking requires that we rescue them from scary situations. And every time we rescue, we perpetuate the belief that they need to be rescued. It also makes them more demanding the next time.

The more reassurance we give, the more reassurance they believe they need. It's never enough, because it's us rather than them doing the work. It becomes a bit of an *If You Give a Mouse a Cookie* kind of phenomenon, where one thing leads to another. We try to use logic. And when she doesn't respond, we try to soothe. Soothing can be helpful, to a point. But we want to make sure we don't catastrophize the situation or get stuck in the soothing phrase.

Her Perception

It's been said that "children are great observers but lousy interpreters."[9] I believe kids with anxiety are even greater observers and lousier interpreters than most others. Remember their negativity bias? When the amygdala becomes hysterical, it overinterprets danger in addition to overestimating the threat. It sees nearly everything as a threat. The false alarm goes off, and your daughter doesn't know not to trust it. She needs your help getting to the truth.

Let me give you an example. I see several girls who have dealt with such severe anxiety that they've developed PTSD types of symptoms with hallucinations. One believed a man had climbed into the backseat of her car and even saw him through the rearview mirror while she was driving. She raced home and ran inside to get her dad. When he went outside, no one was there. It was clear that no one else had been in her car that night.

More common reports I hear pretty much every day from girls include:

"My teacher hates me."
"My friend told me she never wants to be friends with me again!"
"They were all talking bad about me when I walked up at lunch."

These statements may be accurate occasionally. However, worry can cause girls to skew things negatively against themselves, so they can be very black-and-white in their thinking and tend toward the dramatic. They use words such as "always" and "never," and they talk about adults who "hate" them. Certain girls perpetually portray themselves as the victim. They're *always* the ones left out. They're *never* chosen. Their teachers are *out to get them*. The challenge is, if parents are not aware of how anxiety can skew their girl's thinking, they believe her.

Tamar Chansky, in *Freeing Your Child from Anxiety*, writes about helping children change the tracks of the worry train that runs through their brains.[10] When we react to their interpretation of a situation without gathering all of the evidence, we jump on the worry train right beside them. We reinforce the worry.

Evidence is going to be an important tool we'll talk about in the next chapter. But, for now, be wary of picking up the phone to call the teacher. Or the friend's parent. Or even simply reacting in a way that sides only with her view of the situation. Her brain is getting the wrong information from her worries. Anxiety distorts perception. And when that perception is distorted, the problem gets bigger and she gets smaller.

Tools for Her

Anxiety is a lot like a bully. We used to be told that ignoring a bully eventually makes him go away. It doesn't. He only feels more power in the silence. The only way to get rid of a bully is to confront him. Once your daughter learns to turn and face the bully of anxiety, he'll come back less and less often, with less and less power every time. But, first, we've got to go after him where he lives.

Listening to Her Body

Your daughter's worry shows up in her body. It doesn't matter who she is or what she's worried about. When that worry starts to inch its way up her worry thermometer, it registers somewhere in her body first.

In *Braver, Stronger, Smarter*, my activity book for younger girls with anxiety, I provide an outline of a girl at the beginning of the "Help for Me" chapter. It's a little like a body map. I ask her to either write or draw on it her symptoms in the area of her body where those symptoms show up. I always find it fascinating to talk to girls in my office about where they feel anxiety. They usually have a pretty strong sense right away. "I feel a tickle in my tummy," or "My chest starts to hurt," they say. One girl last week told me her hands get sweaty.

The earlier your girl faces the Worry Monster, the less his tricks will work. We want her to understand where worry impacts her body first so that she can recognize the signs right when it starts. And then, she can get to work to shut him down.

Square Breathing

Put your hand on your leg. Really, as you're reading right now. I want you to draw a square on your leg with your index finger. As you make the first line of the square, breathe in through your nose. At the first "corner," pause for three seconds, then breathe out your mouth as you draw the next side of the square. Continue this pattern. Up. Pause. Over. Pause. Down. Pause. Over. Pause. I want you to do that three times. How do you feel now? Any less worried than when you started the exercise? We call this square breathing. And it's the first thing I have any child who worries do.

This past week, I taught a seven-year-old girl square breathing. The square didn't quite have enough flair for her. She asked if she could draw a flower instead. Your daughter may be more of a flower girl. Or she can draw a star or a hexagon, if that's her preference. The great thing about this exercise is that she can do it anywhere . . . at school under her desk, or before a speech, and no one will see her subtle hand movement on her leg. No one will likely hear her deep breathing. It's the breathing that makes the difference, and it's the first tool we want your daughter to have in her worry tool kit.

Deep breathing relaxes the body and slows down the sympathetic nervous system. The blood vessels of the brain dilate, allowing blood to flow back to the prefrontal cortex. The muscles relax. The heart rate slows. The blood pressure begins to stabilize. All of the effects of the false alarm fade away as the body returns to normal and your daughter returns to herself.

Some are skeptical about the benefits of deep breathing. After their daughter saw a CBT specialist, one family told me, "It wasn't that helpful. They mostly just taught her to breathe." Somehow this family missed the message. Learning to breathe deeply is profoundly helpful because of the way it affects her body. However, the timing is important. Deep breathing is helpful when she starts to feel those anxious, tickly types of feelings. If you tell her to breathe when she has already entered the meltdown zone, either it won't work or it will cause even more escalation. "I DON'T WANT TO BREATHE! I DON'T CARE ABOUT THE STUPID SQUARE!" (Can you tell I've heard that one before?)

In addition to square breathing, your daughter can imagine blowing a certain color of air into bubbles or balloons with her breath. Or she can lie on the ground with a stuffed animal on her belly, watching the stuffed animal rise and fall. Regardless of the method, practice with her. We want her to know how to breathe deeply to get her body out of its emergency response status.

Grounding Techniques for Mindfulness

You've probably heard the word *mindfulness* in one place or another over the past few years. Deep breathing is actually a part of mindfulness, which has become a popular therapeutic practice. Mindfulness is used in schools and hospitals all over the world. The Mayo Clinic defines mindfulness as "a type of meditation in which you focus on being intensely aware of what you're sensing and feeling in the moment, without interpretation or judgment. Practicing mindfulness involves breathing methods, guided imagery, and other practices to relax the body and mind and help reduce stress." They go on to say that research has shown it to help with stress, anxiety, depression, insomnia, and physical issues such as hypertension.[11]

As you might expect, mindfulness has its own type of therapy that comes with initials: MBSR. Mindfulness-Based Stress Reduction is a program that was developed at the University of

Massachusetts Medical School and is widely used to treat anxiety. *Forbes* writer Alice Walton says, "A study from Harvard in 2009 found that after an eight-week course of MBSR people had significant reduction in the volume of the amygdala." She adds, "A meta-analysis from Johns Hopkins in 2013 found that meditation was linked to significantly reduced anxiety (and depression and insomnia)."[12]

Before I continue, let me issue a disclaimer, especially if you grew up in the 1970s and 1980s like I did. Back then, most mindfulness practices were attached to the New Age movement, which was popular in those days. You may already be dismissing this as hokey while you picture your daughter in a tie-dyed T-shirt with a crystal hanging from her neck. That is not at all what I am talking about. Mindfulness truly has become a widely successful practice in treating anxiety. I recently referred a young woman to one of the best therapeutic treatment programs for anxiety in the country, and mindfulness was one of the primary methods they used. It works. And although mindfulness has its origins in Eastern philosophies, it can be filled not only with Scripture and prayer, but with the Holy Spirit as well.

Grounding techniques like square breathing are forms of mindfulness. Mindfulness is all about being grounded in the present. Anxiety resides solely in the past or the future. Your daughter starts to worry when she thinks back to something she said that sounded "stupid" to a friend yesterday, or when she jumps ahead to the test coming on Tuesday. She has the worried thought, and then the thought starts to loop . . . and loops again and again and again . . . and we're right back to the one-loop roller coaster at the fair. The more she loops, the more panicked she feels, and the louder the false alarm sounds. A panic attack is at the apex of the faulty alarm system.

When girls describe panic attacks to me, they talk about feeling like they're floating outside of their bodies. In fact, dissociation can be a symptom of anxiety and has been compared to watching oneself in a movie. Grounding techniques are helpful because they really are just what they sound like. They bring your daughter out of her anxiety and right back down to the present.

Many grounding techniques utilize the senses. Square breathing has a double benefit, because it regulates breathing and the act of touching your leg has a grounding effect. Another common grounding exercise is 5-4-3-2-1, where you focus on five things you see, four things you feel, three things you hear, two things you smell, and one thing you taste *in the present*. It helps even more to say those things out loud, if possible, as the sound of your voice also has an added grounding effect.

I mentioned earlier two other grounding techniques I use with girls: the color game, where they name everything they see that is a certain color, and if they are mathematically advanced enough, I also have them count backward from one hundred by sevens, a trick I learned from a psychiatrist friend. Yet another exercise is having a girl think of every word she can that starts with a certain letter, such as *B*.

In essence, grounding techniques help girls focus on something that re-centers their brain and brings them back from the looping thoughts to the present.

Scripture Meditation

God has not given me a spirit of fear, but of power, of love, and a sound mind. Say that sentence—taken from 2 Timothy 1:7—out loud to yourself five times in a calm voice. See the grounding effect Scripture can have? Another thing I do early on in my worry work with girls is ask them to choose a Scripture to memorize on the subject of fear. I have them go home and search through the Bible until they find a verse that brings them comfort. Then I have them say that verse to themselves over and over when they become worried.

It's good for your daughter to find her own verse, although you can direct her to different options. She may need your help memorizing the verse, and she can say it out loud to you when she starts to get anxious. When she repeats the verse, she gets a twofold effect. She not only calms herself by saying it out loud, but she hides God's Word in her heart, and we know Scripture is one of the most powerful tools any of us could have.

Activity

When your daughter starts feeling anxious, the earlier she starts the deep breathing and mindfulness techniques, the better chance they have of helping. But if the worry train has already left the station, if she only digs in her heels rather than breathing with you, and her anxiety escalates, there is one primary method I would suggest: activity.

She may need to move to release some of the tension that has built up in her body before she can turn off the alarm. Have her run up and down the stairs five times. Have her run up and down the driveway. Or have her shoot baskets for ten minutes. Have her jump on the trampoline or get on her bike and ride around the block. Movement resets the body and the brain and can help her get back to a place of calm. She can then practice deep breathing or, if she's ready, move directly to the tools in the next chapter.

Visualization

Let's talk a little bit about bedtime. Most girls tell me that bedtime is the time of day when they are the most worried. If you have a daughter who lies in bed worrying, if she is pre-worrying about and rehearsing all of the things that might trouble her, visualization and progressive muscle relaxation (described below) are two tools I have found very useful over the years with my bedtime worriers.

A mom told me about this exercise that really helped her daughter. When she's lying in bed and can't sleep, her mom lies in bed with her for a set period. The daughter closes her eyes and imagines three doors. Behind each door is a place she loves. In her mind, she opens one door and enters. She describes the scene to her mom, complete with all that she sees and hears (this has a grounding effect). The girl then does the same with the second door and then the third. Her mom told me her daughter doesn't usually make it to the second door, let alone the third, before she falls asleep. But picturing herself in a place she loves has a calming effect, as does saying the words out loud to her mom. Your daughter can do this in school, as well, although she'll probably want to do it silently. Have her think ahead about a place that makes her feel happy and peaceful. And then in moments of stress, she can picture herself in that scene with all of the details she can muster.

Relaxation

Another of my favorite techniques to help kids fall asleep is progressive muscle relaxation. PMR is exactly what it sounds like. Your daughter lies in her bed. She starts at the top of her head and works her way down to her toes, tensing and then relaxing each muscle group for five seconds. The exercise not only relaxes her body but focuses her mind on the muscles and away from her worried thoughts. All of this is based on the "principle of competing demands [which] holds that a person can't be both relaxed and anxious at the same time."[13]

In addition to the following ideas, I highly recommend sitting around the dinner table and having each family member brainstorm their own anxiety-relieving activities to do at home, work, or school.

- Make lists—twenty of her favorite things; ten things she's thankful for; ten people she cares about; etc.
- Remember the words to a song she loves
- Run water over her hands (if she gets anxious in school, she can ask to go to the bathroom and do this)
- Walk
- Swing
- Stretch

- Do cartwheels
- Shuffle playing cards
- Shred paper
- Pop bubble wrap
- Squeeze a stress ball
- Do yoga

Tools for You

Awareness

The more your girl learns about her Worry Monster, the weaker he gets. The more you learn about *your* Worry Monster, the weaker yours gets too. Awareness really is the beginning of change. It's also one of the best tools, now and moving forward, as you help her in her battle. So I want to raise a little more awareness about your own brand of the Worry Monster.

What messages did your parents give you as a child about worries?

What coping strategies did your family use?

How do you handle failure and mistakes?

How do you handle time management? How do you handle your family running late?

What does your child want you to do for her that she can do herself?

What do you do when she wants to avoid something?

How do other family members respond?

Are you modeling anxiety or your own coping strategies?

What is your daughter doing already that might actually be coping skills of her own? (Rituals are sometimes ways kids devise to cope, including bedtime routines.)

What are your most commonly used coping strategies?

You may feel like you need more strategies. The tools in the previous section can be tools for you too. Whether your worry is related to giving a presentation at work or falling asleep, it can impact you in the same way her worries impact her. Your amygdala sounds the false alarm, and your thoughts start to loop. Try square breathing. Memorize a calming Bible verse. Practice mindfulness. As you become more aware and use your own tools, she'll do the same. Coping skills are taught, but they're also caught as she sees you learn to manage your own sense of worry and move back to your own place of calm.

Pursuing Calm

Anxiety left untreated only gets worse. Panic, however, is different. Those intense feelings of anxiety pass with time, usually within five to thirty minutes. If your daughter can hang on, breathing deep and practicing mindfulness, her body will calm down. Your calm in the midst of her chaos helps greatly.

When she starts to escalate, keep your voice level. Do your own breathing. Don't panic. She really will be okay. She may get angry with you in the process, especially if you've been her primary coping skill up until this point. She may want to lure you into an argument so that she can have an emotional release. If exploding at you is the coping skill she uses most often at home, it's one that will continue into adulthood and into her adult relationships, such as her marriage, friendships, and workplace relationships. Teach her healthy coping skills instead. Model them yourself. Pray persistently. Prompt her to practice her skills. She can do this. And you can, too, especially if you both stay calm and connected.

A Strong Connectedness

Your daughter longs to be connected to you. This is a good thing, but not if she uses her worries to feel closer to you. Be aware of the kind of attention you give her when she worries.

I mentioned before a girl who told me her mom was most nurturing to her during panic attacks. She and her mom had a tough relationship with a lot of arguing. When they fought, her mom would lose it. Honestly, I think it took her mom right back to her teenage years and her relationship with her own mom, or lack thereof. And so it was almost as if she became a teenager again. This girl's panic attacks, I believe, were unconscious attempts to make her mom rise up and be mom. She wanted her not only to be connected, but to be stronger in the midst of that connection. The attacks would come at stressful times, but they were always bigger the more she and her mom were having trouble.

We also see plenty of girls in our offices who use their worries to lure in one of their parents. And it's often one parent more than the other. What about your daughter? For moms: Does she tend to cry more if you take her to school than if her dad does? For dads: Does she gravitate more toward you when she's nervous than her mom? If you're the parent she moves toward when fearful, it's possible you're the parent she finds easier to manipulate.

A healthy connection between you and your daughter happens when you help her feel safe. She needs you to always start with empathy—to listen to her and validate her feelings. Then she needs you to help her keep moving, rather than get stuck in the looping thoughts. She needs you to help her use her coping skills and move toward problem-solving her own worries. She'll feel most proud of herself when she's the one who has done the work. When you do the work, she only becomes more dependent on you to do it again the next time. Your daughter is capable. And it's your strong connectedness that gives her the safety and confidence to take on the Worry Monster with her own voice, which is even louder than his.

Intuition

Trust your gut, no matter if you're her mom, dad, or grandparent. You know your girl. You can tell when she's anxious. You know what she needs. Your intuition is one of your greatest gifts to her. It can also be one of your best tools in helping her deal with her worries.

When you know a certain situation is likely going to trigger her, remind her of her breathing. When you can tell she's heading up her worry thermometer, have her say her verse back to you. You may know the Worry Monster is after her even before she does. She's still learning his tricks and doesn't know not to trust her anxious thoughts. You can trust your intuition, as long as you're also living in your own awareness.

Sometimes, you may have to dial down the noise of your own fear to get to your intuition. As you keep working on your worries, your intuition will continue to grow. Your voice will get stronger than the Worry Monster's, just like hers will. Trust yourself and that little voice inside of you. I tell parents daily in my office, "You know her better than anyone in her life. You'll know what to do. Trust your instincts. And pray that they're led by the Holy Spirit." It's what I do as a counselor. I go with my gut and pray often that it's God, not me, who's in charge.

A Balanced Schedule (aka the "Healthy Mind Platter")

The most anxious girls I see are often the busiest. They're the ones who don't have time for what we call "self-care" in my profession. These girls "can't exercise" because of the loads of homework in their backpacks. They can't take a bath, watch a show, or have any kind of downtime because there's "no time" between sports practices and homework and getting in a few hours of sleep. Their schedules are overfull, and so they're overstressed. The thing is, you are the keeper of the family schedule . . . or you can be, whether she likes it or not.

Similar in principle to the food pyramid we studied in elementary or middle school, the healthy mind platter is the creation of Dr. Dan Siegel and Dr. David Rock. It illustrates the "seven daily essential mental activities necessary for optimum mental health," according to Dr. Rock.[14] That's optimum mental health for all of us, not just kids. I believe that these activities not only build resilience and balance, they also ward off worries. They help us grow the connections in our brains, grow our connections with others,[15] and release the stress that builds up throughout our days. They're good for every part of our bodies, minds, and hearts.

A healthy mind platter includes: focus time, play time, connecting time, physical time, time in, down time, and sleep time.

> *Focus time* is time that your daughter spends focusing on specific tasks, which challenge and give her brain opportunities to make connections. Schoolwork would be a primary place for her to have focus time. Learning or practicing a skill is also focus time.
>
> *Play time* is exactly that: play. Play is the "work" of children. It strengthens her problem-solving and cognitive abilities, at the same time decreasing stress. In play, she uses her executive functioning skills in planning the play, and she uses a whole host of other skills, such as adaptability and intentionality, in executing it. It also teaches her to handle frustration and creates more flexibility (which anxious kids need desperately).[16] So play not only lowers her stress in the short-term but teaches her skills to prevent stress in the long-term.
>
> *Connecting time* is time for your daughter to relate to others and the world around her. Relationships strengthen the connections in her brain and help her discover more of who she is. Connecting time can be with family, friends, pets, or nature. All are important to her growing body and mind. (And yes, I believe pets are powerful in the life of a girl for many reasons—see *Are My Kids on Track?* for more on that.) If your daughter is homeschooled, she specifically needs connecting time with kids her age outside of her family. She needs to participate in some type of extracurricular activity through which she's learning the skills

that come with friendship and working as a part of a group of peers.

Physical time is a significant deterrent and antidote to anxiety. Exercise releases endorphins, which are neurotransmitters produced in the brain that reduce pain. Exercise also increases the serotonin in her brain, which is often known as the "happy chemical." Over thirty minutes of exercise yields the greatest results. If she isn't necessarily a huge fan of this portion of her mind platter, you might want to exercise with her. Or a dog can act as your substitute . . . see how helpful those pets can be?

Time in is basically time for your daughter to reflect. This time can include mindfulness but cannot include screens. It's where she has space for the creative and reflective thoughts that kids need to de-stress and to grow. Having quiet time, reading, writing, and creating through art are all examples of time in.

Down time is non-focused time. It's the deliberate doing nothing and "being bored" that might drive you crazy but is a rite of passage for kids. Down time is an important part of children learning to entertain and problem-solve for themselves. It's also often the first to go in a busy schedule. Sixty to 80 percent of the brain's energy is used in the default mode of the brain . . . doing nothing.[17] This time is lying in bed before sleep, relaxing in the bath, sitting on a swing in the yard. Down time recharges the brain's batteries and helps it "store information in more permanent locations, gain perspective, process complicated ideas, and be truly creative. It has also been linked in young people to the development of a strong sense of identity and a capacity for empathy," according to Stixrud and Johnson.[18]

Sleep time is needed for optimal brain growth. Anxiety is worsened by frequent sleep deprivation. The authors of *The Yes Brain* explain, "Adequate sleep is necessary to allow the inevitable toxins of the daytime's neural firing to be cleaned up so we can start the day with a fresh, cleaned-up brain! Sleep is brain hygiene." For all of us. And, if she's not getting enough sleep, you're likely not getting it either.[19]

All of us could benefit from a healthy mind platter. But let's just go ahead and say it. If anyone is going to make sure your family's mind platter is healthy, it's you. You are the keeper of the schedule. You can be the promoter of balance in that. Use the healthy mind platter as an activity around the dinner table. Talk about where you are as a family. What portions are stronger and weaker in your family? What about for each of you individually? And how could you come up with a plan to become more balanced? Spend a weekend with time around each activity, separately and then together, and come back and give a report at Sunday night dinner.

Your amygdalae will thank you. Your bodies will thank you. And, one day, your children will thank you . . . even though they may do a little eye rolling in the meantime.

Dr. William Stixrud and Ned Johnson have done a great deal of research on the high anxiety and low motivation among kids in our culture. In fact, they wrote a book on it called *The Self-Driven Child*. In an interview for *Scientific American*, they talk about it and the need for control.

> Research on motivation has suggested that a strong sense of autonomy is *the* key to developing the healthy self-motivation that allows children and teens to pursue their goals with passion and to enjoy their achievements. But what we see in many of the kids we test or tutor is motivational patterns that are at the extremes of one, an obsessive drive to succeed and two, seeing little point in working hard. Many of these clients say that they feel overwhelmed by the demands placed on them, that they feel tired all the time, and that they don't have enough downtime in their lives (related, in part, to the increasing presence of technology). Many

talk about the expectations that they feel they have to live up to, and many complain about the fact that they have little say over their own lives.[20]

The bottom line, Stixrud and Johnson say, is that kids need "a supportive adult around, they need time to recover from the stressful event, and they need to have a sense of control over their lives."[21] In other words, our kids need us to be strong and connected. They need us to help them learn a sense of balance. And they need us to help them find their way to their own tools to defeat their Worry Monsters. We're going to get to more of those in the next chapter. For now, however, I want you to keep breathing. Help her keep breathing. Remind her that she can do this. You know her better than anyone else does, and you know what she needs.

Yesterday, I met with a little girl for the first time who "leans toward worry," according to her wise mom. As we talked, her mom said, "She's so creative. She just needs some help coming up with tools to manage her worries." What this mom didn't realize was that she had already given her all of the tools her daughter needed. The girl told me about a lava lamp and sensory light her mom had given her. "It really helps me when I'm falling asleep to watch something go up and down and around," she said. Then, she told me how her mom had talked to her about counting sheep. "I hadn't ever tried that. So, I closed my eyes and counted the first one. I thought that I might as well pet it while I was counting. It was so fluffy. I didn't even get to count or pet that many before I fell asleep."

I tried to add on a few more tools—many that we've talked about in this chapter. But, mostly, I told her that the ones she and her mom had come up with together were fantastic. This little girl was already beating her Worry Monster—with all of the creativity and bravery God had placed inside of her and with the support of her connected, intuitive mom.

You've got this. Let's keep moving forward for more tools to defeat that Worry Monster's tricks.

Key Points to Remember

- You are the most important agent for change in helping your daughter fight her Worry Monster.

- Your body has an emergency response system that responds to the fight-or-flight signals from your amygdala. When the alarm sounds, your entire body gets on board.

- The amygdala is notorious for false alarms, especially when you're prone to worry. Your daughter is not thinking clearly when she's anxious.

- Worry impacts every girl's body in different, genuine ways. As a result, she often misinterprets the symptoms as a physical problem and becomes worried about being worried.

- Brains that worry chronically become wired to worry even more.

- The Worry Monster's tricks for you include trying to reason her out of her worries. When reason doesn't work, it's easy to move to emotion and escalation.

- Children with anxiety want certainty, comfort, and reassurance. The more reassurance we give, the more reassurance they believe they need.

- Anxiety distorts your daughter's perception. She needs your help in seeing all sides.

- Physical symptoms are often the first sign she's heading up the worry thermometer.

- Deep breathing calms the body down and lets the amygdala know the alarm was false.

- Anxiety causes her to become disconnected from the present and sometimes her body. Mindfulness and grounding re-centers and refocuses her in the present. Memorizing and reciting Scripture is also anchoring for your daughter's heart.

- Your daughter can't be both relaxed and worried at the same time. Visualization and progressive muscle relaxation can help her body relax, especially at bedtime.
- Coping skills can help your daughter take her emotion toward something constructive.
- Awareness is the beginning of change.
- Your daughter needs the calm, intuitive, strong sense of connectedness that only you can bring. Connect with her, not her worries.
- You are the keeper of the family schedule, and she needs your help in finding balance. Balance includes time to focus, play, connect, reflect, rest, exercise, and do none of the above.

Understanding Yourself and Your Daughter Better

What is her stress level typically? What is yours?

When is the last time your emergency response system kicked into gear? What about your daughter's?

Can you remember a time when your amygdala sent a false alarm? What about your daughter's?

What physical symptoms does your daughter have when she worries? What about you?

What happens when your daughter worries and you try to intervene? What does escalation look like in your house?

Which of the Worry Monster's tricks have you noticed at work in yourself? How?

Where does your daughter's worry affect her first? What about yours?

What is a mindfulness practice you can do with your daughter? For yourself?

What verse has your daughter chosen? What about you?

What have you found that helps your daughter relax? What helps you?

What are some of her coping skills? Yours?

What have you become more aware of since starting this book?

What kind of attention are you giving your daughter when she worries? Do you want to do anything different?

How's your family doing with balance? What would you want to do differently?

5. Help for Her Mind

Anxiety can be sneaky and show up in ways we don't recognize. Yesterday at a conference I spoke with a woman who told me she had just learned that her lifelong stomachaches weren't a medical problem but caused instead by anxiety. She is in her forties, is a mother of five, has written two books, and she's just learning to recognize the Worry Monster for who he is—conniving and relentless. He's relentless, that is, until your daughter learns to face him with the strength and truth of who God made her to be. That's where we're going in this chapter. But first, I'm wondering if you're a little like me, and the Worry Monster is starting to sound like another adversary we know all too well . . .

> Keep a cool head. Stay alert. The Devil is poised to pounce, and would like nothing better than to catch you napping. Keep your guard up. You're not the only ones plunged into these hard times. It's the same with Christians all over the world. So keep a firm grip on the faith. The suffering won't last forever. It won't be long before this generous God who has great plans for us in Christ—eternal and glorious plans they are!—will have you put together and on your feet for good. He gets the last word; yes, he does.
>
> 1 Peter 5:8–11 THE MESSAGE

Christ does indeed get the last word! And I want to keep reminding you and her of that truth—until it's looping in her thoughts more than the words of the Worry Monster.

Now, if you have a very imaginative and very anxious daughter, you might not want to tell her directly that the Worry Monster and Satan sound an awful lot alike. She'd probably become even more anxious and picture Satan hiding under her bed at night. A worry monster sounds a little easier to fight. And we don't want to further the overestimation of the threat. She's got this. Whatever name we use, though, you both need to know the enemy. Or at least you need to know his tactics—against her and against you.

The Worry Monster's Tricks for Her

> If you know the enemy and know yourself, you need not fear the result of a hundred battles.
>
> —Sun Tzu[1]

Let's go back to your daughter's brain for a moment. When the false alarm of the amygdala sounds, the prefrontal cortex tries to find and solve the problem. When there is no real threat, the prefrontal cortex uses its vast powers of imagination. In other words, the amygdala has sent your daughter's body into fight-or-flight. But the prefrontal cortex now sends her mind into endless exaggerated, catastrophic what-if kinds of possibilities.

As we covered in the last chapter, the first battlefront is her body. The second is her mind.

When the Worry Monster sounds the alarm, your daughter believes she's in danger. It can take fifteen to twenty minutes for her body to calm back down and for the fight-or-flight response to subside. Her thinking is not clear until it does. In those moments, the Worry Monster has the advantage and uses it. Remember from the beginning of chapter 4, the amygdala takes less than half a second to spring into action. And when it does, those worried thoughts come right behind it.

What are those thoughts? Her worries typically fall under one, if not all, of these categories.

Exaggerated Likelihood

There is no "slight chance of rain" with a worrier. There is a 100 percent chance of rain. Every. Single. Time. And it doesn't matter what the fear is. That fear has already shifted to predestined fact.

I will throw up at school today.

I will have a panic attack at the track meet.

My mom will have a car accident.

My friends will laugh at me if I wear that outfit.

I don't know about you, but I was an expert worrier when I was growing up. Especially when I was trying to fall asleep at night. I can picture myself in my room, lying there . . . hearing every random thump and creak and noise of the house. I still remember seeing in my mind—and the image felt way too real—the people who had already killed my mom and dad in their sleep and were headed up the stairs to kill me. I wasn't just worried about it; I was certain of it. And so is your daughter, whatever her fear is. That Worry Monster takes the thing she's most afraid of and convinces her, through her worried brain, that it will soon be a horrible, terrible fact.

Catastrophic Thinking

Almost ten years ago, I counseled a very conscientious sixth-grade girl. She wanted to be a good student in every way: She did *all* of her homework *all* of the time, she studied *thoroughly* for tests, she came to class *prepared*, she raised her hand *every* chance she could. Can you hear the anxiety building? She wanted her teacher to believe she was smart, hardworking, and honest. And, somewhere, in all of the pressure she was putting on herself, she developed a fear of cheating.

I remember a story she told me one day. "I was sitting in class today working on a quiz," she said, "and I looked up toward my friend who sat in front of me. I wasn't trying to cheat, but I saw the edge of her quiz. I didn't see any answers, but I got really worried. I started thinking about how I didn't mean to cheat, but maybe I saw something unknowingly and cheated by accident. I thought, *Oh no, I may have cheated.* And so I went up and told my teacher I just cheated on my quiz."

Did you notice the looping thoughts? The panic? The amygdala taking over and the logic going out the window? At first, the girl was confident she hadn't seen any answers. But by the end of the worried train of thought, she was convinced she had cheated and she even confessed to her teacher.

Since that time, I have heard some version of that story probably twenty different times. With catastrophic thinking, the worst thing is not only going to happen, but it will be even worse than she expected when it does happen!

"I will throw up at school today, and everyone is going to see me, and then I'll have to go home and change, and my desk will be empty, and everyone will know what happened and laugh at me all day long."

"I will have a panic attack at the track meet. Max, who I like, will be there and see it. He'll think I'm dumb and weird and won't ever like me!"

"My mom will have a car accident and die, because I didn't say good-bye to her one more time."

"My friends will laugh at me if I wear that outfit. They'll even say something rude about me on social media or edit me out of the photo. They won't invite me next time. They probably won't even want to be my friends anymore. Maybe they never liked me to begin with."

And so it loops . . . and loops . . . and loops. And what's even worse is that these girls believe they're helpless to stop the thoughts.

Underestimated Ability

One exercise in cognitive behavioral therapy is to have the client draw a circle. Within that circle, they write or draw pictures of the things they can control. Outside of the circle, they draw the things they can't control. I see too many girls who believe that nothing controllable exists within their circles. This sense of powerlessness has become a hallmark of girls with anxiety. There's nothing she can do to change, she thinks. She's not brave enough. Or strong enough. Or smart enough. (Therein lies the title for the girls' activity book.)

If your daughter is a worrier, somewhere along the way she has adopted faulty views of herself. As I said before, girls are hard on themselves. Maybe she's a perfectionist and makes negative comments about herself. Comments from other girls are sometimes more hurtful. So throughout her growing-up years, your daughter has likely heard hurtful comments that have seeped down into what she believes about herself. Regardless, if you hear her starting sentences with "I can't," "I don't know how," "I'll never be able to," or "Everyone else," you have a window into the Worry Monster's attacks on the girl you love. She's not only doubting her abilities—she's doubting herself.

It's true she may not be able to control her situation, but she *can* control how she responds to it. Each and every time. But she may need you to help her remember.

A Faulty Memory

Worry has no memory. Well, to be accurate, it has no memory of the good or brave things—the times your daughter fought and beat the Worry Monster before. Instead, it remembers every bad thing that happens to your daughter and uses only those memories in its algorithm for probability. Good experiences are never taken into account. It's like a debit and credit system, except no credits build up in the land of anxiety—only debits.

What this means is, when your daughter gets anxious, she doesn't remember the brave thing she did yesterday. She doesn't remember that school was actually fine once she got inside the building. She doesn't remember the time she said her line in the play flawlessly and even had fun. She doesn't remember the times she felt confident and proud of herself. She can't celebrate her victories over the Worry Monster, because she can't remember them. She can only remember his tricks.

Study after study has found that negative events affect us more than positive ones. It's hardwired into the way our brains process emotions and memories. A *New York Times* reporter interviewed Clifford Nass, professor of communication at Stanford University, and summarized Nass's observations: "Negative emotions generally involve more thinking, and the information is processed more thoroughly than positive ones. . . . Thus, we tend to ruminate more about unpleasant events—and use stronger words to describe them—than happy ones."[2] Dr. Nass was describing grown-ups with fully developed brains. We're talking about the girl you love who is still growing—the girl who skews things against herself, whose brain isn't fully developed and has an amygdala that both overreacts and underestimates. Typically, girls with faulty memory ask lots of questions.

Perpetual Questions

Several years ago at Hopetown, our summer experience for kids, one girl in particular was struggling with anxiety. She asked a question (or more) practically on the half hour *every half hour* she was awake. "What are we doing next?" "What time is lunch?" "When are we going on the lake?" "What time is bedtime?" "What time are we getting up in the morning?" It was exhausting. As I mentioned in the last chapter, children with anxiety want comfort and certainty, and they want it perpetually. She wanted to know what was happening next. She wanted to know right then. And again thirty minutes later. Hopetown is tightly run, but to the kids it probably looks laid back, and flexibility is terrifying to a girl who worries. (We'll come back later to the idea that it's also an important life skill for her to grow in.)

How many questions does your daughter ask in a day? Does she ask repeated questions about the same things? In her book *Why Smart Kids Worry*, Allison Edwards suggests a Five Question Rule, allowing your child to only ask five questions on the same subject per day.[3] Your daughter is asking questions for reassurance. She wants comfort and certainty. She trusts you. And she asks. And asks. And asks again.

In case *your* worries are now kicking in—What should I do? What am I supposed to do when she asks so many questions? How do I stop her from asking so many questions? Why is she asking the questions in the first place? How do I know when she's truly wondering about something or if it's her worries sparking the questions? (Was that five questions?)—I'm going to provide a couple of tools here in the middle of discussing the Worry Monster's tricks.

If your daughter asks something repeatedly, give her a limit. "You can only ask five questions about the same subject. Make sure your questions count." She'll automatically *slow down* and *think*—which is the last thing the Worry Monster wants her to do. The panic will often pass just in the process of her having to think about which questions she really does want answered. You can also turn the question-asking back on her. "How long does it normally take me to make your breakfast? So, when do you think we'll be eating?" You can even empathize and ask open-ended questions about her worries. "Sounds like you're starting to feel some fear about that. What do you think you're afraid of?" And my favorite tool is just to confront the Worry Monster head-on: "Is that your worry talking, or is it you?"

I need to prepare you, though: If you've been answering her constant questions up to this point, you've been giving the mouse a cookie, so to speak. When you stop, that mouse—and that Worry Monster—is going to get *mad*! We'll talk more about what are referred to as "extinction bursts" in the next chapter. Suffice it to say, she needs coping mechanisms other than you. And questions are one of the Worry Monster's biggest tricks on you both.

The Worry Monster's Tricks for You

I've already mentioned how *her* reassurance seeking is one of the biggest tricks of *your* Worry Monster. You can easily fall into the trap of trying to reassure her catastrophic and exaggerated thinking. But reassurance always needs more reassurance. The mouse needs more cookies. She gets louder and often angrier. And then we have another problem on our hands.

Allowing Bad Behavior

In therapeutic circles, anger is considered a secondary emotion because there is often another emotion lying underneath the anger. Anxiety is often the primary emotion that leads to anger for girls. And boys, too, by the way. Younger girls, in particular, often don't have the understanding or words to describe what they're feeling. So when parents of toddler-age girls come to my office to talk about anger they're seeing in their girl, many times we end up talking about anxiety.

Anger comes out differently for every child. Whether they explode or implode, are wired for worry or struggle with negativity, or have experienced trauma, all children who worry a lot seek comfort and certainty. They don't feel much of either inside of themselves. They cling to safety, which often includes you. They ask what-if questions and can become demanding if the answers don't take away their intensifying anxiety. They want to know their schedule for the entire day when it hasn't even started yet. They avoid new things and new people and do their best to avoid whatever makes them most anxious. For many, their anxiety comes out with you more than with anyone else, because you are the safest thing in their lives. Your daughter can cry the entire way to school, and then pull it together in front of her teacher. She can keep her worries in check in front of her friends, but then she gets in the car with you and falls apart. Because you are safe, you get the brunt of the safety- and security-seeking behavior.

Anxious kids are overly focused on their own emotions and their own needs. Out of that awareness, they can get demanding, particularly of you.

If your daughter's worries and demands come out in the form of anger, she still needs discipline. In every parenting seminar my colleagues and I teach, we talk about how boundaries create security in kids. She will feel safer when she knows she's not the most powerful person in the room. Boundaries also build confidence. If she's allowed to get away with being the worst version of herself, she eventually becomes who she believes she is.

You can start with a warning: "I know you're angry, but you're not allowed to talk to me that way." Or, "I can tell that's your worry talking, but I want you to breathe for a minute and try to say that again more respectfully." Give her a warning first, as she may not know she sounds angry or disrespectful in the moment. Then give her consequences if she doesn't rein it in. If her anger goes unchecked at home, it will eventually spill over into school and friendships and future relationships.

Connecting the Dots for Her

Another of my favorite things to talk about at parenting seminars is the magic formula of empathy and questions: "That sounds really hard. What do you want to do about it?" "I can tell the Worry Monster is trying to get at you right now." "What is the Worry Monster telling you? Does that sound right to you? Which of his tricks do you think he's trying to play on you?"

Resist the urge to connect the worry dots for your daughter—to tell her how anxiety is affecting her or fix her worry for her. If you connect the dots for her, she'll need you to keep doing so. Remember, she longs to be independent. You want her to learn problem-solving skills. You want her to learn to use the thinking part of her brain, as that's the part that can defeat the Worry Monster. Telling her to stop worrying doesn't work. Teaching her to think for herself does. (We'll come back to this in the following sections.) When anxiety strikes your daughter, ask questions and offer empathy instead of connecting the dots, and she'll learn problem solving and find confidence along the way.

Content Trap

Another way the Worry Monster tries to bait us involves the content of her worries. "I'm afraid the dog is going to bite me!" she might yell to you. The most natural response in the world is to reassure her that the dog is nice, he would never bite her, and so on. Then, when her whac-a-mole worries resurface on another topic, say, your safety while you run errands, it's tempting to answer that one with, "I'm going to be fine. Nothing is going to happen to me while I'm away from you." All this is called the content trap. We hit the dog-biting mole and then the traffic-accident mole pops up. Then another and another in different spots. (I'm sincerely hoping you've played the arcade game Whac-A-Mole so that you know what in the world I'm talking about.) The problem is not the dog or the accident or any other subject her worry will attach to over the years. The problem is the worry itself. And we need to equip her with tools to fight the worry directly.

Tools for Her

Expect Worry

In this world, you will have trouble. (Chapter 7 centers around this very idea.) But I want to emphasize here that because your daughter is prone to worry, one of the most important tools for her is to expect that worry will raise its head on a regular basis. We want her to learn to expect it, particularly in certain situations.

If she struggles with social anxiety, she will worry on Sunday nights before school starts back up on Monday. If she has separation anxiety, she'll worry before you leave town. If she has any kind of anxiety, nights can be tough when her mind isn't otherwise occupied. We want her not only to expect worry, but to be prepared for it with a box full of tools to defeat the Worry Monster when he predictably circles back around. Your daughter has certain times and certain situations that trigger her worry. The more she anticipates those triggers, the more quickly she can catch the thoughts once those triggers are set.

Name the Thoughts

You may have heard the phrase, "The first thought isn't the right thought." In the twelve-step recovery world, it's boiled down to "first thought wrong." Regardless, the truth behind the phrase definitely fits worry and anxiety. The first thought is often the anxious thought, and that first thought comes quickly, as we've said before. We want the girls we love to learn to catch the thoughts as they come, particularly the anxious thoughts, and even give them an appropriate name. The recovery community also calls it stinkin' thinkin'. We could call it worried wisdom—although there is nothing wise about it.

Which thinking mistakes is your girl most prone to making? We want her to recognize the Worry Monster's voice, and then separate that voice from her own. Giving him a name is part of what separates him from her, and his voice from hers.

You can make it fun with her. She doesn't have to call him the Worry Monster. She can name him something else. If she's a teenager, she can name it something that sounds a little cooler and more teenager-y. I'm working with a young girl right now who named him Bob. Have her give him a voice like Mickey Mouse or Donald Duck. She can draw a picture of him with a silly face or funny hair. It's easier to fight the monster outside of you than inside. And so naming him and learning to recognize his voice makes him easier to fight—it brings him down to her level so she can level him with a few more tools of her own.

Find the Evidence

I've had more teenage girls talk about wanting to be crime scene investigators in the last ten years than ever before. Little do they know that Nancy Drew has had the corner on that market since the 1930s, inspiring generations of would-be girl detectives. Whether your girl is six or sixteen, she can follow the threads and find the evidence—or lack thereof—disproving the Worry Monster's claims. He plays on fear rather than fact; possibility instead of probability. He tries to convince her that something that happened once will happen always. He's got her number on the overexaggerations and underestimations, as well as the black-and-white thinking that's still normal for her age.

So we want her to look for evidence that not only disproves him but proves her bravery. We want her to start with the worried thought and figure out the following:

- What is the negative outcome she's afraid will happen?
- How many times has the negative outcome actually happened in the past?
- How bad would it be if that outcome happened? What would happen next? How bad would that really be? (Keep going until she gets to the end and sees that she would still be okay.)
- When was a time she was brave recently?
- When was a time she took on the Worry Monster and did the particular thing she's worried about?
- What evidence proves the Worry Monster's theory that she can't do it?
- What evidence proves the "Brave Theory" that she *can*—that she's more capable than she knows?

The Brave Theory is where we want her to land—it says she's capable and strong and that God has already given her all that she needs. She can do the scary thing. We know the evidence proves it, and, as she works out the tools in the next chapter, she will too. But, first, we want her to do a little CSI work and find the evidence.

Just last week I met with a high school freshman whom I'm having do a little detective work of her own. She has social anxiety. Her anxiety has impacted her thinking about the past and future. She thinks her friends will decide they don't really like her, as she believes has happened many times before. She doesn't think she has friends, although she has plenty. She skews things against herself and believes the worst possible outcome will inevitably happen. So, I talked to her about observer bias—about how research says that we basically find what we're looking for. If she's looking for evidence that her friends don't like her, that's what she's most likely to find. Any sideways glance from a friend in the hall will prove her theory . . . or the Worry Monster's: that they're not interested in what she has to say and not even interested in being her friends. If, however, she's looking for evidence to prove that they do like her, then that's what she's most likely to find instead.

I know this girl well. I know she will find evidence that she is liked by her friends, because I know they do like her. I like her too. She's just currently using her detective skills to benefit the Worry Monster rather than her own brave self. It's time to do something different. And it's time to get a little bossy in the process.

Boss Back

Girls can be experts at being bossy. Your most worried girl can wag that finger and put her hand on her hip with the best of them as she tells her little brother—or even the dog—how he's supposed to behave. We want her to channel her bossiest self with the Worry Monster.

Typically, girls talk to themselves in a way that exacerbates their fear, especially when their amygdala is in control. *"You can't do this." "You're terrible at that." "Last time you did it, you looked so silly." "They're all watching."* That self-critical voice comes so naturally for her. Dr. Tamar Chansky calls it her "worry brain."[4]

Scientists have observed that our brains get better at whatever they practice. This phenomenon is called neuroplasticity. So at this point, however old she is, she's likely mastered the art of the worry brain. Instead, we want her to develop mastery over using her thinking brain to "boss back" the worries.[5]

It starts with calming her body down enough so that the amygdala is no longer in control. Then, when she's once again using her thinking brain, we want to engage it in the fight against her worries. "Worry Monster, you're not the boss of me! I'm not listening to you anymore!" And, then, she can remind herself of all of the reasons that he is flat-out *wrong*.

"We have an alarm system, so I would know if someone tried to break into my house. So would my parents, and so would the police!" was one girl's message to her Worry Monster in my office recently. It sometimes takes a little practice, but being sassy is pretty fun when she's allowed to be. She can say it in a silly voice. She can sing it in a rap song. She can stick out her tongue and stomp all around the house as she says it. But we want her to use her words and her voice to boss that Worry Monster back. We want her to use her smart brain against her worry brain. The more she uses her voice to boss the Worry Monster back, the more she, in turn, builds up that voice, as well as her confidence and the neuroplasticity in her strong, smart brain.

Worry Time

A CBT tool that helps put boundaries around anxiety is called *containment*. If you're a fan of the TV show *This Is Us*, you might have seen containment in action. Do you remember the scene where Randall and Beth are riding in the car and the subject of worries comes up? They each say one sentence about their worst fears about their daughters, starting with Deja.

> Randall: "Deja never turns this around and ends up in jail. Go!"
> Beth: "She might kill us both in our sleep. Go!"
> Randall: "She might kill us both not in our sleep. Go!"[6]

Their back and forth goes on for a few minutes, but then they're done. That's all the time and energy they're allowing worry to have. They've contained the anxiety.

It will hopefully look a little different for your daughter (no murdering types of fears involved). But the idea is that you create some method for her to contain her anxiety and set it aside until a certain time of day. She can have a "worry box" or "worry jar." She could put it in her phone if she's older. Basically, whenever an idea comes up that worries her, she contains it until her "worry time." The worry time is predetermined and has a beginning and an ending time; it's typically fifteen minutes long at most. If she has anxious questions for you, don't answer until her worry time. You can answer any of her "what-ifs" then. Listen, offer empathy, and remind her of the tools she can use to fight the Worry Monster.

It will be hard for your daughter to wait until worry time. But every time she does, she learns that she can control her worries. She's stronger than they are. And often, during the waiting, the catastrophic thoughts will get a little smaller and the exaggerated likelihood will get a little less likely. She'll return to reason and to herself. You can even increase the wait until her worry time, having her flex that muscle of control. Don't wait until bedtime, however, because talking about her worries then will have her looping right to sleep. Or not sleeping.

Her Voice

In the twenty-five-plus years I've been counseling girls, one of the most important and hallowed parts of my work has been helping girls find their voices. In this day and time, it feels more important than ever. Because there are foes without and foes within, including the Worry Monster, she needs to both know and learn to use her voice. She needs to know what she believes and how to express it. One of the things we say at Daystar—and to kids all over the country—is a quote by our friend Dan Allender: "You are the only you this world will know, and something about your life is meant to make something about God known in a way no one else can do."[7] No one will know that *something* the girl you love can bring to the world until she learns to use her voice.

Have her practice. Encourage her to strengthen her voice just like the other "muscles" we've been talking about in this book. When you're out to dinner, have her order for herself. Don't ask for the ketchup for her; let her ask. Have her call and order the pizza from time to time. I know college-age girls who are terrified to pick up the phone and call Papa John's. Ask her questions. Ask her opinion on current events. Have her say her thoughts on a movie you've seen or a sermon you've heard before you share your ideas. She needs practice finding and using her voice. Even if she doesn't yet know it herself, even if she doesn't have an answer, the fact that you asked means you not only want to hear but that you value who she is and what she has to say.

Tools for You

I spoke at an event yesterday and felt like I botched it. It started with a comment made by an attendee right before I began my talk. She didn't mean anything by it, but she brought up something that feels like a particularly vulnerable spot for me. The problem was, it didn't hit me at the time. But it clearly took me off my game. I just didn't realize it till much later, when the looping thoughts and my own Worry Monster had taken over. So let me tell you what happened. Actually, let me tell you two versions of what happened: what happened in my head and what it would have looked like from your perspective had you been with me.

It was a talk called "Navigating the Relational World of Kids." It's a new talk, which means I haven't quite gotten my groove down yet. I feel a little unsure if it's the *most* helpful material I can give the audience, which is, obviously, what I want. (Perfectionist alert—already setting myself up.) But it's got a lot of practical strategies for making, keeping, and being a friend. What any parent wants, right? Well, not this crowd—not from my vantage point, anyway.

I started talking about how, from their earliest stages, boys communicate to establish rank. They play games of competition. Someone wins. Someone loses. And someone often goes to jail or dies before it's all over (you know, cops and robbers and the like). Girls, on the other hand, communicate to connect. They play games of inclusion, where everyone has a role, things like house and school. Every man in the room looked annoyed. *Uh-oh.* I started to panic inside. Then I told a personal story I don't usually tell that I thought was kind of funny in a self-deprecating sort of way. But they seemed to feel sorry for me instead. Every person in the room, by that point, either looked irritated or was smiling at me like they would at a fourth grader who had dropped their notes during a speech in class. I couldn't finish the talk fast enough. Then, at the end, when I prayed, I think I closed the prayer twice, finally spluttering out, "In Jesus' name. Amen." But what almost came out of my mouth was "In Jesus' name. Good-bye." Literally. I almost said "Good-bye" instead of "Amen." I felt terrible the entire rest of the day. I couldn't get it out of my head, and I woke up the next day with it still on my mind—thus, these paragraphs.

I've decided that maybe I don't really like writing books, since God seems to keep trying to give me real-life examples of what I'm writing about at the time. The chirping amygdala smoke alarm was enough. But anxious, looping, self-critical thoughts are *no fun!* Here's what I realized in my early-morning, not-yet-awake thoughts: This is exactly what happens to your worried daughter.

If you were sitting with me in the room, this is what I believe the situation would have really looked like. Those poor folks had been listening to speakers for three days at this conference. I was the last in a long line of big voices and funny stories. I'm a little bit more understated of a personality and like to connect with the faces of the people in the room, no matter how large that room is. I was in a terrible location at the conference center. The room felt like your Psychology 101 classroom, with awful lighting. The attendees had just come back from lunch and had full bellies and exhausted brains, I'm sure. I think they were just happy to sit. Those who were awake were with me from the first moment. Granted, some people may not have been as emotionally invested in that particular topic. That's okay. It's pretty normal that a few tune out during any speech. Others looked a little disgruntled when I talked about ways any of us can still inherently struggle as grown-ups. But I address that in every talk, because I feel like it's something we all need to hear. And the gratitude for insight usually outweighs the discomfort of the information. But the majority of the people in the room smiled and laughed. Several asked questions at the end. Several others came up and were grateful. And as I was waiting on the car to take me to the airport, someone approached to ask how they could bring us to their church for a parenting conference. Sounds like a successful event. But I couldn't get there in my own mind. I needed help. Your daughter does too.

The Worry Monster is waging a serious war on the battlefront of her mind. It's debilitating (take it from me). And you actually know what it's like too. You have a thousand stories like the one I just told. It's almost impossible to get out of those looping, self-critical, worried thoughts on our own. She needs your help.

When it comes to anxiety-fighting tools for her body, you can prompt and remind her, but she truly has to do it on her own. You can't regulate her amygdala. But you can help her shift her thoughts. In fact, I want you to be very involved in the beginning stages of her learning the tools we just talked about in her section. Then, the more she puts them into practice, the more I want you to step back. She's going to gradually take ownership of the process. But, at least in the beginning, her tools in this section are yours too.

You know by this point that she's going to struggle with worry. She doesn't know that. She doesn't remember. And, without help, it will catch her by surprise every time. Anticipate her triggers. She also doesn't know that other children worry. She thinks she's the only one who went home from the conference feeling bad about herself. (Oops, that was me.) She's not the only one, but she'll be even harder on herself believing that she is. Help her understand that other children worry too. She's certainly not alone in her battle against the Worry Monster. You're with her, and you're keeping an eye on the worry and how it affects her mind.

Watch the Worry

I often sit with parents who talk about how their daughters go from zero to ten in seconds. They're right—as I said earlier, it takes less than a second for the worried thoughts to come. It feels even faster to her than it does to you. But there is a specific cycle her worries take. Her thoughts affect her feelings, which affect her behaviors. We want to study and learn that cycle so we can help her do the same.

How does it start for your daughter? Maybe, on Sunday night, you're helping her choose which clothes to wear on Monday morning. She doesn't like your first choice, and suddenly, she's in a full-scale meltdown. When she is, you're often the first casualty. She gets bigger and bigger in both volume and escalation. She brings up all of the things that have gone "wrong" in the past week—many of them things you've done because you're the "worst mom" or "worst dad." She jumps from subject to subject, trying to think of anything to draw you into the fray. She becomes like a drowning person, trying to cling to you to save her, only to take you down in the process.

Something has happened to trigger her worry cycle. She needs you to help her figure out what. **Step back and ask yourself what is going on.** She's not in her thinking brain. Why not? What could she be worried about? **Have her breathe and do her mindfulness exercises. Get her moving,** if she can't move from her worried thoughts. **Distract her with a question.** "Guess who I ran into today?" She'll have to think about your question, rather than her worries. In CBT, it's called changing the channel. **Then, when she's calm, go back and talk to her.** "I think that old worry got to you today." Ask questions about what she thinks happened. Don't lecture. She can tune out your lecture, but not your questions. **Help her put words to her emotions.**

Molly, our Daystar art therapist, has kids draw volcanoes. She has them write what thoughts and feelings they have as their emotions escalate inside the volcano to the point it erupts. "A scary new situation happens. . . . I feel frustrated. . . . I get out of control." And then, on the outside of the volcano, the things that help them calm down, such as square breathing (when the scary situation happens) and bossing back the Worry Monster (when they feel frustrated). Then they write the consequence at the top (when they get out of control and the volcano blows). You get the picture. Draw a volcano with your daughter. Draw one for yourself. Help her see on paper the progression of her own worries. It may be that an eruption for her involves tears more than anger. But either way, she needs to understand the cycle her worry takes. She needs to be able to track how her thoughts affect her feelings, which affect her behavior.

I would suggest a worry journal that you keep for your daughter. In the activity book *Braver, Stronger, Smarter*, I also ask girls to keep a worry journal. After she's been particularly worried, write about it. What was she worried about? On a 1 to 10 scale, how significant did the worry seem? What thoughts and feelings was she communicating? How did that affect her behavior? What helped her calm down? As you start to track her worries, you'll notice both what makes her worry worse and what helps. You'll be better educated to help her and, eventually, give her even more ownership of the fight. Until you can understand the progression her worry takes, worry will have the upper hand with her and with you.

Watch Your Response

When anxiety comes after your daughter's mind, it's maddening for you both. You want to reason with her. You want to comfort her. And she's coming at you swinging. Or she's coming at you with endless questions. Or a feeling of being overwhelmed that you just can't seem to make go away. In those times, your response is important. She needs a few things in particular from you:

She needs warmth. Children who suffer from anxiety, studies show, have parents who struggle to offer warmth. They aren't as affectionate, don't smile as often, and have what counselors would call a flat or negative affect, according to Chansky.[8] I get it. I meet these very parents in my office on a regular basis. They're not cold; they're tired and frustrated. You probably are too. She still needs your warmth. According to the research of Daniel Siegel, attunement is one of the best predictors of self-regulation in children.[9] Attunement is a combination of both your warmth and understanding. Those two characteristics not only help her calm the volcano back down, but they help remind her that she's safe and loved in the midst of the volcano. She wants to please you, even when her volcano is erupting. When she feels that she's not, by observing either your response or your face, she'll become even more anxious.

She needs understanding. Her worries are going to be frustrating for you both. But they're real. She is worried. The bigger the emotional eruption, the bigger the worry. She needs you to take her seriously but not her worries. "Is that your worry talking or you?" "That sounds like the Worry Monster to me. I want to hear your voice, rather than his." She needs you to listen to her worries with warmth. She needs you to offer compassion and empathy. She needs you to do your best to understand how her worries are impacting her—and not for the sole purpose of fixing them. For the purpose of attunement, so that she can learn to self-regulate. Remember what happens if you're the one who fixes them? You'll just need to fix them again. And she'll never learn the tools herself.

She needs perspective. Song of Songs 2:15 says, "Catch for us
the little foxes, the little foxes that ruin the vineyards." In
the Bible, vineyards are symbolic of joy. Melissa taught on
little foxes years ago at Hopetown. Since then, it's become
a part of our staff vernacular. "That was a little fox" is our
way of saying there is some annoying little thing that's
feeling bigger than it should right now. We all have little
foxes, and it helps to call them by name. Worry is definitely a little fox that feels like a BIG fox to your daughter.
She needs help putting that worry into perspective. You
can use the fox analogy, or you could use words like "little
worry," "medium worry," or "giant worry" to help her describe how much a situation is affecting her at the time.
The Worry Monster is a magician at enlarging thoughts
and feelings, and it will help her immensely when you
teach her the art of perspective.

She needs confidence. No matter where your daughter is
right this moment—upstairs asleep, sitting in class, spending the night at her grandparents'; no matter if she's five
or if she's fifteen; no matter where she is on the worry
spectrum—one of the most important things for her is to
find her voice. She can't do it without you. Ask her questions. Elicit her opinions. Show confidence in who she is
and who she's becoming. Give her responsibilities at home
(yes, even chores). When you give her responsibilities,
you're reminding her that she's capable of fulfilling those
responsibilities. She *is* capable. Chores are actually empowering for kids! Help her find her way to purpose too. When
she gives of herself, she'll experience not only a sense of
fulfillment but also a sense of confidence. Confidence and
anxiety are antithetical to each other. Now, don't confuse
confidence with arrogance. I know plenty of girls who are
arrogant and entitled who actually feel more anxious because they're bigger than they need to be. But confidence

helps her feel empowered and more sure of herself. When she's confident within the safety of your warm, understanding relationship, she'll feel more ready to take on the Worry Monster and whatever he brings her way.

Help Her Practice

Every one of these tools for your daughter will be like a muscle. She'll need practice growing that muscle just like she would any other. We'll talk more about it in the next chapter, but it's okay for her to feel uncomfortable. In fact, I'm going to tell you to let her be a little uncomfortable on purpose—a little fox version of uncomfortable. She has to learn to work through the worries. She has to practice finding the evidence and bossing the Worry Monster back. Keep practicing with her. Make it fun. Role-play with her and her worries using silly voices or dolls or stuffed animals. When you do, don't forget to use positive self-talk. In fact, make sure you're modeling positive self-talk in your own life. She'll need to practice in the midst of feeling unsure and uncomfortable. She'll need to watch you do the same. Life and the Worry Monster are going to throw a lot of unsure and uncomfortable at her.

> For though we live in the world, we do not wage war as the world does. The weapons we fight with are not the weapons of the world. On the contrary, they have divine power to demolish strongholds. We demolish arguments and every pretension that sets itself up against the knowledge of God, and we take captive every thought to make it obedient to Christ.
>
> 2 Corinthians 10:3–5

The enemy, whether we call him the Worry Monster or Satan, is going to come at her with a lot of unsure and unpredictable moments, as well as a lot of arguments, most of those directed at her thoughts. With God's help, she can demolish every argument that he sets up against the knowledge of God—and the knowledge of who she is in Christ.

As you watch her battle the Worry Monster, let her be the expert. You begin the process by teaching her the tools. But as she puts them into practice, let her teach you what she's learning. Sit down with her at some point each day and let her tell you where she's felt brave or like she's made a step against the Worry Monster. Any step is progress in this fight. Any step is a step toward her confidence and her empowerment and her freedom from worry. She can do this. God is going to have the last word, and He's going to use her brave, strong, and smart voice to do it.

Key Points to Remember

- The first place the Worry Monster attacks is her body. The second is her mind.
- The more we learn about the Worry Monster, the weaker he gets. The more we listen to him, the stronger he gets.
- He has several tactics he uses most often in his attacks on her mind: exaggerated likelihood, catastrophic thinking, underestimated ability, faulty memory, and perpetual questions.
- Worry has no memory and assumes the worst . . . about the situation and her.
- Give a limit to her questions. She'll have to slow down and think, and the panic will have time to pass.
- Anxiety often comes out as anger in girls. And your girl takes her anger out on you. When she's allowed to get away with being the worst version of herself, that's who she believes she is.
- Your daughter needs help practicing problem solving and experiencing independence. Questions and empathy help.

- The content trap is when we fall into responding to the specifics of her worry, rather than the worry itself. It's one of the Worry Monster's biggest tricks on you.
- The more your daughter learns to recognize what triggers her worry, the more quickly she can stop the worried thoughts.
- She needs to name her Worry Monster in order to take away his power.
- She needs your help learning to catch the thoughts, find the evidence, and then boss the Worry Monster back when the worried thoughts come.
- Bossing her worries back involves teaching her thinking brain to overpower her worry brain.
- Creating worry time helps her learn to contain her anxiety, teaches her that she can actually control it, and often gives it time to subside on its own.
- Her voice is one of her most important assets in her war against the Worry Monster and in life. She needs your help in using it and valuing it when she does.
- All worry has a cycle. Your daughter needs you to be a student of hers and to come alongside her in it with understanding, warmth, perspective, and confidence. She also needs practice.

Understanding Yourself and Your Daughter Better

How have you seen the Worry Monster try to outsmart your daughter? How has he tried to outsmart you?

Does your daughter lean toward exaggerated likelihood or catastrophic thinking? When is a time you saw one or the other recently? Which do you lean toward?

How do you see your daughter underestimate her ability?

When was a time you saw your daughter take a positive step in her war against worry that you could remind her of?

Does your daughter get angry when she worries? How have you handled her behavior in the past? How could you handle it differently in the future?

How can you stop connecting the dots for your daughter and help her learn more problem-solving skills?

What content trap has your daughter fallen into? How can you change the script when you respond?

Practice finding evidence with a worrisome situation in your life right now. What evidence proves the Worry Monster theory? What evidence proves the Brave Theory?

Practice bossing her Worry Monster back. Find a situation that you can role-play this. How did you feel as a result? What about her?

Brainstorm with her about worry time. Where could she store her worries? When would she like the time to be? How does she think having a worry time might help?

How can you help your daughter develop her own voice today?

What is your daughter's worry cycle? What is yours?

How do you typically respond to her worries? How could you respond differently?

How can you help her practice this week?

6. Help for Her Heart

The first place the Worry Monster is going to come after your daughter is her body.

The second is her mind.

The third is her heart and the choices she makes out of that heart.

He wants to discourage her. He wants her to feel incapable. And one of the best ways to accomplish his plan is to make her believe she can't _____ [fill in the blank]. As clinical psychologist Dawn Huebner says, the Worry Monster is a genius at making "easy things seem hard, and hard things impossible."[1] His genius is rooted in your daughter's fear, her perfectionism, and her insecurity. He's also a master of sabotage.

He'll make her miss a day of school because her stomach happens to hurt on a Monday morning. Then, she'll feel a little funny about going back the next day, but she'll do it, with lots of coaxing from you. The next Sunday night, she feels nauseated again, so she misses Monday. When she hasn't gone for three Mondays in a row, there's no way she can go on the field trip the following Monday. She starts to worry about the birthday party on Friday night, since she feels out of the loop with her friends from missing the field trip. It gets harder and harder each morning to get her out of the car at school. It no longer works to have the school counselor walk in with her. Soon, you find yourself contemplating homeschool, and she finds herself disconnected, discouraged, and disheartened. She gets angry at herself and at you every time you try to force her to do anything.

What do you do?

If it was your own fear, you'd likely push through it. But with her, you're worried you'll make her feel worse. When you were younger and anxious, your mom made you push through. It was awful. You want so much for your daughter to feel understood and safe. So maybe if she just takes a little break. . . .

The problem is, you also want your daughter to go on school field trips. You want her to know how to do things like order her own meal at a restaurant. You want her to have the experiences of being away from home and going to summer camp. You know she really does need to be with other kids. She's spending more time hiding in her room, or hiding behind you. And while it's nice to have the time with her, something inside of you keeps saying that things are getting worse.

Avoidance strengthens anxiety. That sounds intense, I know. But I wholeheartedly believe it is true, which means . . . **she's just going to have to do the scary thing.** When you make all the scary things go away for her, it sends a message to her that she can't handle them. Rescuing communicates that she needs rescuing. That the problems are too big and she is too small, which is the opposite of what you want her to hear.

Here's what I want your daughter to hear: *You're going to feel uncomfortable sometimes. You're going to worry. You're going to feel awkward, and you're going to be afraid. Everyone feels those things every day. Even the girls who look confident and seem secure. As my friend Melissa says, bravery exists in the presence of fear, not the absence of it. You are stronger than your worries. You are smart enough to solve any problem life throws at you. And you are brave enough to do more than you can imagine.*

That's what this chapter is all about—not only teaching her but allowing her to experience what conquering her scary things in small, manageable doses feels like. But first, let's talk about the tricks the Worry Monster will try to use to stop her. And you.

The Worry Monster's Tricks for Her

Several years ago, a mom told me about the time when she and her husband surprised their kids with a trip to Disney World. Their sons whooped and hollered when they heard the news. Their daughter was not so thrilled. Let me clarify: Their daughter who struggled with worries was not so thrilled. When her mom and dad met her at school with packed suitcases, a pair of Mickey Mouse ears, and a MagicBand, she burst into tears. "What? Disney? We can't go to Disney! *I didn't know, and I'm not ready!*" And then she went on to explain her logic. "I didn't have a chance to tell my stuffed animals good-bye, and they'll be so worried when I don't come home from school today! There is no way I can go to Disney!"

First of all, I love her compassionate heart toward her stuffed animals. However, her desire for predictability—her demand for predictability—would have caused her to miss a memory-making adventure with her family. She would have missed it, that is, if her parents had fallen for one of the Worry Monster's primary tricks for her. . . .

Predictability

Transitions are hard for children who lean toward worry—transitions of any kind. If a child comes from a divorced home, transitioning back and forth from Mom to Dad can be tough and disruptive emotionally. For a child with anxiety, however, even transitioning from homework to bath time can be difficult. She craves predictability because it feels safe. And she always has a plan, whether you know it or not. She has an idea of where she thinks things are going and when. When you disrupt her plan to ask her to take out the trash or get ready for bed, her worry is triggered. And because those transition times are often linked to something you've asked her to do, her response can look more like disobedience than anxiety. She dissolves into tears or an angry outburst, or she flat-out refuses.

I'm working with an elementary-aged girl now who gets in trouble at school almost every day for being "disobedient" to her teacher. When her teacher tells her to stop her work, whether it's for lunch or recess, she keeps writing. When we talked about it in my office, she told me she wants to make sure she gets every answer right. She doesn't want to put down her pencil until she has completely finished her worksheet. It doesn't sound like disobedience to me. It sounds much more like worry in the form of perfectionism. And her teacher is missing her heart when she dismisses it as defiance—and only making the anxiety worse.

Your worried child craves predictability. She wants to work within the system of what she expects and the plan she has decided makes her feel safe. To put it even more accurately, it is the Worry Monster that craves predictability. The more you give in to his demands for predictability, the more your daughter and your entire family will end up living by those restrictive demands. We don't want to play by his rules.

Comfort

According to researchers, the primary difference between generalized anxiety disorder (GAD) and obsessive-compulsive disorder (OCD) is the presence of compulsions or ritualized behaviors.[2] Those who struggle with GAD and those who struggle with OCD have similar looping thoughts. Both can become pretty obsessive. But individuals who suffer from OCD develop rituals to make themselves feel better.

If I wash my hands enough times, I won't get sick.

If I lock and relock my doors twice, no one will be able to break in.

If I say the same things in the same order at bedtime, the monsters won't crawl out from under my bed and get me.

Rituals are also known as safety behaviors. Now, every child or adult who engages in safety behaviors isn't necessarily dealing with obsessive-compulsive disorder. Anxiety can still be true anxiety and have obsessive-compulsive-like symptoms. But the goal is still the same: comfort. Your daughter wants you to say "I love you" three times before she gets out of the car before school. It brings her comfort in the midst of her fearful, looping thoughts. She also thinks that somehow there is a link between that behavior and your safety. In her mind, you magically won't die if you say the statement three times. If you don't say it at all or only say it twice, there's just no telling what might happen.

Last year, I was at dinner with a friend and saw a couple whose daughter I was counseling. They told me they had left her at home, much to her tearful dismay. Their daughter was thirteen, plenty old enough to be home alone for a few hours in the evening, but she had already texted her mom seventeen times in the ten minutes they had been at the restaurant. I hear similar stories in my office constantly. Parents talk about going on neighborhood walks and getting panicky texts the entire time from their kid at home. Technology use can be a safety behavior for your child, just like the rituals that she creates to bring comfort.

The problem with rituals is that they strengthen the worry more than they strengthen your child. They give her both the predictability and comfort she craves. And they lead to an even greater need for control.

Control

Anxious children are some of the most controlling children I counsel. It's not that they necessarily mean to be. It's just that taking control "fixes" the problem, at least temporarily. They create rituals and set up systems that make them feel safe, but the downside comes when those rituals are disrupted. You probably see this in your own home. Even though it may add some extra time to your evening, it's far easier to go through her required routine of kisses and comments at bedtime than to manage her volcanic emotional eruptions. We abdicate to keep her happy or our home peaceful or sometimes because we simply don't know it's a problem.

I talked to an adorable girl yesterday who has anxiety. She is kind and responsive and has about the closest to perfect manners of any fourth-grader I've ever known. She is smart, capable, and a delight to be around. But her need for control is overtaking her life and the lives of her family members—or at least the lives of her siblings.

I've known her parents since she was a toddler, when they noticed a bit of concerning behavior. At three, she was so worried about making her bed in the morning that she would wake up in the middle of the night, quietly smooth her sheets and arrange her pillows until they looked just right, and then fall back to sleep on top of her comforter. Several years and three siblings later, her desire for control has only gotten stronger. And those siblings are a huge wrench in her system, particularly her little brother. He actually relishes being a wrench in her system. He makes the family late for school almost every day because he doesn't want to stop playing or has gotten his clothes dirty already and has to change. You can imagine how being late for school goes over for this little girl. *Hate* is not quite strong enough a word. She has recently started choosing his clothes and laying them out for him the night before. She told me yesterday that when her siblings make a mess, she has to clean it up because she doesn't feel "okay" until things look right again. The problem is that, with four children in the family, things likely aren't going to look right for the next fifteen years.

A major component of anxiety is the need to take control.[3] Individuals who have anxiety really believe that being in control is the answer. It fixes the problem—that is, until the next safety behavior is needed.

Soon, *your daughter learns to trust the safety behaviors more than she trusts herself.* Her need for control becomes problematic in that, rather than her learning to control her anxiety, the anxiety controls her. Until she learns to recognize the Worry Monster and the lies he's telling her, she will be forced to obey his demands. She'll have to work harder and harder to clean up after her brother. She'll have to wash her hands more often at school. Or check that the doors are locked one more time before she goes to bed. She won't learn flexibility. She'll be dependent on her safety behaviors to maintain control. And she'll only feel comfortable when she is fully in control, which we know, as adults, isn't what real life looks like very often.

Questions

Girls who worry often have an endless supply of ready-loaded questions.

"What if my friend isn't there?"
"What are we doing next?"
"What if they laugh at me?"
"What if I can't do it?"
"Will I have to ride the bus tomorrow?"

I met with a family recently who told me that, every night, before she falls asleep, their daughter asks if she has to ride the bus tomorrow. She has been riding the bus every single day for four years. In effect, the question has become a safety behavior for her. And her parents' affirmative answer has become a part of her routine. Seems harmless enough, right? But the truth is, the questions only make her worry stronger. Answers are much like reassurance with a worrier; they only require more answers. It's never enough. Or the answer never seems to hold. Instead of us falling into the content trap and answering, she needs us to respond back with questions.

"Is that your worry talking or you?"
"How have you gotten to school every day this year? What do you want to say back to your Worry Monster?"
"How did you beat the Worry Monster last time he tried to come at you with the what-ifs?"

She needs to connect the dots and boss back the worries. We want to hear her strong voice more than ours, and certainly more than the voice of her Worry Monster.

Avoidance

In my office, if there is one primary trap I see families fall into, it's avoidance. Girls demand and parents comply. And the Worry Monster wins twice over.

I had a couple in my office this week who said, "We just don't know how much to push." I get it. Parents don't want to make their anxious daughters feel bad. You don't want to create more anxiety than there already is. She's sure not saying, "Mom and Dad, I'm scared, but I know this is good for me." Her amygdala is on the loose, and she's in a full-blown, raging, tearful meltdown. Sometimes you're just too tired to put up a fight.

What was something that was important to your daughter but she avoided? How did she feel about it afterward?

I worked with a girl for years whose primary trigger was being away from home. She was terrified of overnight field trips and church retreats. Her one exception was our summer camp, because, as she said, it was "the only place I can go away from home and feel safe." Until it wasn't.

Because anxiety has boomed into a childhood epidemic in the past few years, we're still learning what helps the most therapeutically. I'll admit I have fallen for many of the Worry Monster's tricks myself over the years. I coaxed this girl to go on trips. I stepped into the content trap and talked about how she had close friends who were going and how fun trips would be. I reassured her. Every once in a while she would go—but, more often than not, she'd give in to the Worry Monster and stay home. Whenever she did, his voice just got louder. When she finally decided she couldn't go to summer camp any longer, I thought, *Okay. She'll miss camp one year and regret her choice. She'll see photos of her friends having fun and won't miss camp again.* The problem was that she did regret it. She was sad about missing the fun and even felt some degree of shame for not being able to spend a week away from her mom and dad as a teenager. But she never came back to camp. Anxiety doesn't have a memory, remember? So believing she was going to learn from that mistake was just me falling into the trap of avoidance as well. She regretfully stayed home, and *the safety she felt was stronger than her regret.* The Worry Monster just flexed his muscle that much more.

That girl needed to do the scary thing. And so does your daughter. Avoidance not only strengthens anxiety, but it makes her feel worse about herself along the way. Bridget Flynn Walker says, "Avoidance . . . reinforces your child's fear and actually causes it to grow and spread." She goes on to cite psychologist Michael Tompkins, who describes "reducing avoidance as the primary way to conquer all fear and anxiety."[4] Your daughter needs to be pushed—not too far, but past the predictability, comfort, and control that the Worry Monster promises will keep her safe. She will learn to fight the anxiety and feel better about herself every time she moves past avoidance and steps forward in bravery.

The Worry Monster's Tricks for You

Accommodating

"I'm afraid I've bubble-wrapped her since she was little." The wise parent sitting in my office owned her part in her daughter's avoidance. The mom was accommodating, rescuing her from facing certain situations.

Rescuing your daughter limits her likelihood to learn, explain the authors of *The Yes Brain.*[5] When you make accommodations for her, allowing her to avoid certain situations, you encourage dependence more than independence. Independence makes her feel good about herself. Dependence makes her feel insecure.

"Hi, I'm Sissy. I'm so glad you're here. Let me show you around, and then I want you to come upstairs and meet my little dog, Lucy."

This is what I say to every child who comes in for an assessment at Daystar. Usually, the warmth and coziness of the Daystar house has already put them at ease. When I smile, they typically smile right back. When I mention Lucy, game over. Nine out of every ten children come upstairs with me, a stranger, without once looking back over their shoulder at their parents. The one out of ten is typically a young child with anxiety who is struggling specifically with separation from her parents.

An eight-year-old girl came to Daystar for that reason recently. I was expecting her to be anxious, based on the notes from her mom's initial phone call. When I met her, however, her smile was wide, and she popped right up from her chair to follow me. Her mom, before she walked away, grabbed her wrist. "Do you feel comfortable with that?" she asked. Immediately, this little girl's face fell. Honestly, she was fine until her mom asked that question. Her mom followed us up the stairs and sat right outside my door, rather than in the usual downstairs waiting room. She asked her daughter if she was comfortable four more times in the fifty minutes we spent together for the assessment. She was being accommodating.

Other accommodations can include asking the school for certain types of help, or pressuring camp leaders to let their daughter call home every night before bed—despite the camp's no-call rule established because they've learned that kids are more homesick when they call home. (Can you tell I've had that one before?) Research says that the more parents accommodate an anxious child, the more significant her symptoms will be.

"Parental accommodation," writes Walker, "is an extensively studied and well-documented phenomenon in families with children suffering from anxiety disorders, and the higher the level of parental accommodation, the poorer the treatment outcome tends to be."[6] In other words, when you accommodate your child's anxiety, you give the Worry Monster more power and take away your daughter's power.

As a therapist, however, I have seen times when certain accommodations were necessary *for a targeted period of time.* For example, I have seen girls whose panic or medical symptoms were so severe that they simply couldn't go to school. Their parents, with the help of the school *and* mental health professionals, took them out of school for a specific window of time. They used the time in counseling to work on coping skills for both the girls and the parents. Then the girls gradually reentered school, going for longer and longer time slots each week.

Any temporary accommodations need to be just that—temporary. They need to include a weaning-off plan, both for your daughter and for you. A counselor can help you devise an objective plan to lessen the accommodations and strengthen her (and your) ability to cope.

Working Harder Than She Does

One of the best pieces of advice I've ever heard as a counselor is that you can't care more than someone else does about their own problems. More than twenty-five years in, I still find myself doing it all the time. I want so much for the child I'm counseling. I push and encourage and cheer and push more, only to meet even more resistance. At that point, I usually (hopefully) realize that I have landed in the "caring more zone." The more I care, the less she does. She either becomes lazy, letting me do the work, or oppositional and reactive, as in she's a teenager.

I tell parents the same statement often: You can't care more than she does about her grades, about her hurt over a ruptured friendship, you name it. With grades, you can always impose consequences when the grades fall below a certain point. But when you have more emotion over something in her life than she does, she typically either shuts down or simply stops talking to you about it. Worry operates under the same idea. You can't work harder than she does to defeat her Worry Monster.

"When parents work harder than their kids to solve their problems, their kids get weaker, not stronger," write Stixrud and Johnson.[7] To defeat her worries, your daughter will have to learn problem solving. She'll have to calm her body, shift her thinking, and use her own coping skills. You have tools to help, but it is the process of her using her own tools that strengthens her body, mind, and heart.

Tools for Her

Emotional Vocabulary

When my colleagues and I travel and speak, we take our books with us, but we also take an adorable feelings chart designed by our friend Katie. You can buy feelings charts online or at any local parent-teacher store. (There's also one in *Braver, Stronger, Smarter.*) The charts typically show faces with different expressions that represent feelings, including happy, sad, angry, embarrassed, and so on. We travel with feelings charts because we believe every family should have one. Or more. We know many families who have bought several—one for the car, one to put on the fridge, one for their child's room that can be pulled out at bedtime. I use one daily in my office.

Last week, I asked a seven-year-old girl who came in for worries to point to and name three feelings she felt regularly. She chose happy, proud, and, of course, worried. I asked if she ever felt angry. "No." "Do you ever feel sad?" I asked. "Is that the same as worried?" was her question back to me. My guess is that, for her, it is.

I meet with another girl who worries from time to time. Most recently, I saw her after she took a vacation and experienced an episode of severe anxiety. The more we talked, the more I discovered that she was feeling left out by her favorite cousins over the course of that trip. She was sad and hurt, and lonely, and it was all manifesting as anxiety.

I see a high school girl with pretty severe anxiety, who also happens to be exceedingly kind. She was bullied for years before I met her. Different girls had bullied her. Different situations.

Different schools, even. But one thing remained the same: She didn't know how to stand up for herself. She felt hurt, then very appropriately angry at how she was being treated. But she had no idea how to express that anger and still be the kind person she longed to be.

Girls who worry are not only some of the smartest kids I meet, they're also some of the kindest. The most thoughtful. The most compliant. And they're some of the least likely to talk about their feelings. All of the sadness, hurt, disappointment, and even anger come out as worry. Worry is more appropriate, in their minds. It won't make anyone else feel bad, they think. And the more they press down those feelings, the stronger the anxiety gets.

In our book *Are My Kids on Track?* the first emotional milestone we talk about is an emotional vocabulary. It's where every child needs to start. We want to give kids the tools to talk about their feelings and to talk about them with the words that accurately describe them. Anger is a feeling; it's only a sin when we hurt others out of that anger (Ephesians 4:26). Sadness is another very appropriate emotion, as are frustration and embarrassment and confusion and a whole host of other emotions that are underneath the worry that so many girls experience.

With girls I counsel, I have them choose three faces from the feelings chart, and then we talk about grass. More specifically, we talk about the dirt underneath grass. What we see on the surface of a girl's life—green, growing grass—is evidence that there's something underneath (aka dirt). And in that "dirt" are lots of different feelings that are important to talk about. We need to help the girls we love use words that act as garden spades to dig underneath and discover more of what they're truly feeling. We need to help them express those feelings so that they don't all spill out as worry. The Worry Monster would love nothing more. He'll take all of the worry that her other emotions can muster, and then he'll use it to keep her from doing the very things that defeat it.

Exposure Therapy

Exposure therapy is one of the cornerstones of cognitive behavioral therapy.[8] Developed in the 1950s, exposure therapy gradually teaches people to do scary things—the things that trigger anxiety and fear—in a not-so-scary way. According to the American Psychological Association, therapists "create a safe environment in which to 'expose' individuals to the things they fear and avoid. The exposure to the feared objects, activities or situations in a safe environment helps reduce fear and decrease avoidance."[9] So it reduces the fear, but the person still has to do the scary thing.

Speaking of which, I've lived in Nashville for almost three decades. I love this city, though I must say it's getting too big for my small-town Arkansas roots. Still, there is only one thing I don't love about Nashville: cicadas. I'm sure you've seen cicadas before. They're those gross-looking, flying insects that make a loud screeching sound and leave their shells on trees in the summer. It wouldn't be so bad if we had regular cicadas and in regular amounts, but we have *cicadas*. As in, I keep waiting for Moses to put his staff in the water and turn the Tennessee River to blood when they come around. It is like a plague. And I am not exaggerating. Fortunately, they only descend on Nashville every thirteen years. And, every thirteen years, I seriously consider moving back to Arkansas, where they don't live or pass through.

Right before the last plague (I mean, infestation; I mean, appearance), I had a fifth-grade girl come in for anxiety. She knew the cicadas were coming and was terrified. (I couldn't really tell her that I was, too, and there might be another therapist better equipped and less cicada avoidant.) Anyway, she was afraid and sitting in my office, so we had to go with it.

For her exposure therapy, we started off talking about the cicadas. Just talking about them, in the beginning, made her nervous. The next step was having her draw pictures of cicadas with silly faces or in pajamas. Then, we looked at photos of them online. We made a game of it, where she would say a silly word, turn quickly to look at a photo of a cicada, and then turn quickly away. Eventually, we watched videos of actual cicadas on YouTube. She gradually became more and more exposed to the dreaded things, and, as she did, her anxiety level declined. By the time the cicadas arrived, they were still yucky and a little scary, but their presence was not debilitating. And she was extremely proud of herself for learning to manage her fear. (I, however, was still running from my house to the car in a hooded raincoat.)

If your daughter is using the *Braver, Stronger, Smarter* activity book, I provide a drawing of a ladder to help her understand and use exposure therapy. At the top of that ladder she should indicate a specific goal, such as spending the night at a friend's or grandparent's home. Then, on each rung of the ladder, she'll write a step toward that goal. The ultimate goal is for her to learn to keep going even when she's afraid, no matter which ladder step she happens to be on at the time. Your daughter may push back. She would most likely rather try when she doesn't feel fear. But any of us who have made it to adulthood know that's not the way life works. Her behavior changes first, and then her thoughts and feelings follow suit. "Ninety percent of the pain associated with anxiety occurs *before* the exposure to anxiety-provoking situations or experiences. Anxiety is a disorder of anticipation," say the authors of *The Anxiety Cure for Kids*.[10]

Your daughter can climb any ladder she sets up for herself and tackle any specific fear, as long as she does it gradually and with support from you. As you're helping her come up with her goals, two types of exposure therapy can help: imaginal exposures and in vivo exposures. Imaginal is exactly what it sounds like. She imagines herself doing the scary thing before she begins to practice doing it. She can imagine herself at a friend's house—picturing step by step what will happen, starting with walking through her friend's door, while she practices relaxation techniques. Just picturing the steps in her imagination will start to alleviate her fear and raise her comfort level with the idea. Her imagination is a great place to begin with any exposure ladder or in any anxiety-inducing situation.

Next, we move to in vivo, or real-life, exposures. We want to continue to work our way up the ladder of worry. If she's afraid of throwing up, for example, she could play with fake vomit first. (Yes, it actually can be purchased.) She can then move on to make silly throwing-up sounds, or your entire family can with her. (I know—sounds like a lot, doesn't it? But it always helps to make a game of it.) She can also have a stuffed animal participate in the exposures. If she's afraid of meeting someone new, her stuffed animal can meet the person first (although you might have to prepare the person for a stuffed animal encounter). She can have a supportive person come with her, on one rung of her ladder, before she moves to doing the scary thing alone. Exposures can also include drawing pictures of herself doing whatever makes her afraid, or even taking a silly test about the particular fear-inducing subject.

There are a million ways she can work herself up the ladder of exposures. She can do it in her imagination as well as in real life. As she moves forward, she needs to remember to breathe and use the techniques we've talked about, such as mindfulness and bossing her worries back. But the bottom line is that she has to keep moving and doing the work. She needs practice moving forward in courage, and it's the practice that really does instill in her the belief that she can.

Practice

The more worried your daughter is, the more confidence she gains from accomplishing the task. And that kind of confidence is exactly what you want for her. You want her to know that, even when she's worried, she has coping skills. She can beat the Worry Monster. But she only beats him when she fights. And to fight well, she's got to build up those monster-fighting muscles. Practice is the weight training of worry work. And a lack of practice is the primary reason kids don't defeat their Worry Monsters.

Once she completes one rung on her ladder, she needs to do that thing over and over and over. She needs to do it until her worry thermometer goes back to normal. Then, she needs to tackle the next rung of the ladder. If one rung is allowing herself to be in a scary situation, she needs to stay in that situation for at least five to ten minutes. She needs to stay long enough to let the initial spike of worry pass. It's a little like going into cold water at the beach. She wades in a little, gets used to it, wades in a little more, and so on, until she's swimming like a brave, worry-fighting fish.

Here's a real-life example: If your daughter is struggling with school-based avoidance and has been missing school for a period of time, she needs exposure therapy in gradual steps. Enlist the school's help and maybe have her go for her first two classes for two weeks and then until lunch for the next two weeks, until she has worked her way toward a full day of school.

I will say, having her work through her worries may bring up your own worries. *Can she do it? Am I pushing too hard?* I get the same questions in my office regularly. Pushing her without tools would be too much. It would feel defeating. But pushing her with the tools to do the scary thing is just enough. It's empowering. She can do it. She is capable. And she's got everything she needs inside of herself, with the tools that you're adding to her problem-solving tool bag.

Problem Solving

We're so busy being the resources for kids that they don't develop resourcefulness. We talk a lot about problem solving in our chapter on resourcefulness in *Are My Kids on Track?* It might be another chicken-or-the-egg situation, though, because I also see a determination on the parent's part to solve the problems for her. I'm sure it's unintentional, but anxious children often rely on others to handle hard situations for them. It's important to note that research shows that anxiety is related not to a lack of problem-solving skills, but a lack of confidence in problem-solving abilities.[11]

If you find yourself stepping in and doing the work for her, she'll step out. She'll step out in fear. Or demandingness. Or sometimes even laziness. Regardless, she'll step out. She'll trust your voice more than she trusts hers. She needs to strengthen her own voice as well as her own problem-solving abilities. She's going to have more than a few problems along the way, and you want her to learn to think for herself and trust in her own strength when those problems arise.

In *Anxious Kids, Anxious Parents*, the authors discuss how "teaching kids to problem solve reduces the chance that they'll develop an anxiety disorder."[12] Have your daughter make a list of things she's good at. Remind her of problems she's solved in the past. Ask her questions. If she says, "I don't know" or "I can't" when a problem arises, go back to that magic formula of empathy and questions.

"What do you think will help?"

"What do you believe is the best thing to do?"

"I think you're a great problem solver."

Every time you ask her questions and encourage her to solve the problem on her own, it reinforces that you believe in her. Your questions for and confidence in your daughter strengthen her voice *and* her problem-solving, worry-fighting muscles.

Tools for You

Ownership and Collaboration

"She needs other tools. The ones you gave her just aren't working." I have heard this from parents countless times over the years. What I've come to realize is that the tools are not working because the child is not using them, or it's a halfhearted effort when she's already in full-blown meltdown mode. She will not do the work unless she buys in to the work—unless she believes the work will help, and you believe in and with her. Rewards help a lot (which I'll discuss in the next section). But ownership is where we want to start.

Your daughter needs things she has ownership over that have nothing to do with worry. One idea? Chores. As soon as she can walk, she can clean up one toy at a time in the playroom. She can carry her little plate to the table. As she gets older, she needs responsibilities that are not allowance earners but ones that come just as part of being a member of your family. She needs to carry her own backpack and pull her own little roller bag through the airport, even if it seems bigger than she is. She needs ownership and responsibility. Ownership not only builds confidence in girls, it also builds buy-in. Remember, she wants to be independent. She feels proud of herself based on your belief and her experience.

Ownership means she takes the lead. Collaboration means you're there to support. Your job is to ask questions. To believe she can do it. To be understanding and to be tough at the same time. Her job is to defeat the Worry Monster. In fact, we really want her to be the expert on worry.

When I meet with girls who worry, we go over a lot of skills in their sessions. At the end of each session, I have the parents join us to review the skills she's learned. I have her teach her parents what she can do to fight worry. They ask questions and she answers, rather than me. In teaching them about worry, she experiences using her voice and she feels proud of herself for being the one in charge. It helps reinforce what your daughter is learning to teach someone else what they should do if they worry, no matter if it's you, a stuffed animal, or even her dog. Regardless, we want her to see herself as the expert on worry and overcoming worry.

After she teaches you, then you get to step in with collaboration. When she comes up with her ladder plan, for example, ask her about it. "What is your goal? How can I support you? What part of this can you do on your own?" We want to ask questions in a collaborative way. We want to give her choices in her fight against the Worry Monster. Letting her make choices gives her a feeling of being in control at a time when she not only needs it, but doesn't feel very much of it.

She may want to rely more on you than herself when things get tough, but don't fall for it. If she asks for help, ask a question back. "What part of this can you do on your own? How can I help you accomplish that?" If you feel tempted to help when she hasn't asked or when she can almost do the task, step back. Remind her that you want to help her and not her Worry Monster. You can even tell her that your Worry Monster has kicked into gear and is telling you that you should take over the fight. You're going to have to fight him in your way, and she's going to have to fight hers in her way. But it's her work—her ownership with your collaboration—that makes the difference in her own life and her own battle against him.

Praise and Rewards

I try really hard not to be black-and-white. It's a tendency for us type A, one on the Enneagram people. But I'm about to be. When your daughter is working on her anxiety, she needs you to encourage *every* effort *every* time. She needs you to be excited with and for her. She needs you to notice when she makes a step, any step. She wants you to be proud of her. Your response is one of the best rewards she can get. Tangible rewards help too. And when the two of you collaboratively come up with a system of rewards, her buy-in and her results are that much greater.

Each effort needs to come with an immediate reward. For younger girls, especially, you can use points, marbles, or any other small item. I'm a fan of something visual girls can see in their rooms. Most often these days, girls choose those brightly colored, fuzzy pompons. They look fun in a jar on her dresser, and she can watch the number of pompons grow, seeing before her eyes her progress against the Worry Monster.

Here's how it works: She earns a point or pompon for every exposure or every time she's brave. She then collects pompons to turn them in for a preselected reward. You can come up with the list of rewards together, with different rewards worth different numbers of points. The bigger the reward, the more points it's worth. She can save up rewards for a big one, or choose small rewards more frequently.

Here are some basic guidelines when it comes to rewards:

- The younger she is, the more frequent the rewards should be.
- Don't take away points as punishment. She could end up owing you pompons and feeling more discouraged than when she started the system to begin with.
- The rewards can be based on repetition, but not consecutive days. Having to repeat a task every day in a row can feel like too much pressure for a child who already feels a lot. For example, she gets a bigger reward when she sleeps in her own bed for five nights, whenever those five nights come, rather than five nights in a row.
- Include celebrations as part of the rewards, particularly if she accomplishes one of her bigger goals.
- It typically takes three weeks to establish new behavior.

As far as what works best for rewards, her input is invaluable. Before she starts her exposure work, sit down and talk about things that would incentivize her. She'll likely come up with a few (or more) items that require money.

Tangible rewards can undoubtedly be motivating, such as a book, stuffed animal, toy, a new song or game, or an item she's been wanting for a long time. But rewards don't have to cost anything—your time is actually one of the best rewards. Going for a bike ride, playing a game, having lunch or dinner at a fun restaurant of her choice, going on a picnic, and getting to choose and watch a family movie can all be rewards that involve relationship. Other favorite options of girls I see include ordering pizza, taking a bubble bath, having a later bedtime, and planning and having a sleepover. Whatever the reward, it needs to be one that is both meaningful and motivating for your worried girl.

A word of warning about siblings: They may get jealous. However, I often tell parents that each child can have their own jar of marbles. Each adult can, too, in reality, because every one of us has something we need to work on. It may not be that her brother needs to work on bravery. But there is certainly a muscle he could benefit from developing and working on toward his own system of rewards: patience or self-control, for example. Each family member can have their own motivation and their own reward options.

As a parent, whatever you give attention to in her life is, in essence, what you reward. If you give more attention to her anxiety and panic, her anxiety and panic will increase. If you give more attention to her bravery, her bravery will grow. Again, we want to be both understanding and tough in the collaboration. This journey is going to be challenging for her. It's going to take time, a lot of effort, and a lot of courage.

Rewards will not only help her buy in, but they will also help this process feel a lot more fun. Listen to, praise, and reward *every* attempt on her part to work through her worries. Focus on her coping skills and independent behavior. Believe in and remind her of her bravery. She won't remember or believe it for herself many times along the way. She'll need you to consistently remember, remind her, and praise even the littlest steps.

Consistency

Just as practice is a crucial tool in her fight against the Worry Monster, consistency is a crucial tool in yours. And consistency may sometimes cause a fight *with* her when her Worry Monster has taken over. Whether her fight is with the Worry Monster or with you as you try to help, she needs you to be consistent in your rewards, in your support, and in your strength.

An extinction burst is a phenomenon that occurs for many kids in the beginning of the process. It's a little like an alcoholic binge-drinking the night before rehab. Her behavior may get a little worse in the beginning—or the Worry Monster's behavior, that is. There may be more anger, more questions, more tears. Stay consistent. The Worry Monster doesn't go down easily. But your consistency will pay off over time.

Anxious children live by the once-and-done rule. After they screw up their courage to accomplish a task once, they may dig in their heels and say (loudly) that they "ALREADY DID IT!" They want independence, but they're afraid. They have anxiety, after all, so doing the scary thing over and over can get hard. And tiring. She needs to do the scary thing over and over—until it no longer feels like the scary thing. She needs you to stay consistent through the process. Keep cheering her on every single step of the way. She can do this and so can you.

Flexibility

Yet another important tool against worry is flexibility. As we seek out uncertainty and discomfort on purpose, we reduce anxiety and its effects. Flexibility and the amygdala have an inverse relationship. The more we strengthen the muscle of flexibility, the more we quiet down the amygdala. Flexibility literally resets the amygdala and cuts the number of false alarms, according to the authors of *Anxious Kids, Anxious Parents*.[13]

How can you develop more flexibility as a family, especially with an anxious daughter? First, it can be helpful to practice in the safety of your own home. Change seats at the dinner table. Serve breakfast for dinner. Make beds with the pillows in the opposite direction. Mix up the bedtime routine or which one of you wakes the kids in the morning. Little changes can have a big impact on your daughter learning flexibility.

Your child, like all of us, will face discomfort throughout her lifetime. She will live with uncertainty and even disappointment when things aren't what she expects. When you practice flexibility as a family, she learns that she can feel safe and uncomfortable at the same time. She's still okay. She can still cope. She is still herself in the midst of the scary and uncertain things. As Wilson and Lyons say, "Fear, uncertainty, discomfort, worry . . . are normal and expected parts of life and are signs that you are moving forward, stepping into life, and growing."[14] Your daughter is growing, even if the steps feel small and slow. Any step is a step of courage and of bravery for her. Encourage her. Celebrate with her. Remind her often of all that she's accomplished thus far in her fight against the Worry Monster.

As you've read this chapter, you may have come up with your own ladder of personal goals. My hope is that your primary goal is to teach your daughter to be *herself*—to have her own voice, to discover her own confidence, to develop her own problem-solving skills. She needs your collaboration in this process. She needs you to help her discover who God has made her to be. That is the version of her you want to help launch into the world. The version that has good judgment, that learns to discern God's voice and to follow where she believes He's leading her. That's the version of her that can learn not only to live with uncertainty, but to be brave and strong and smart in the midst of it.

First John 3:20 in *The Message* says, "For God is greater than our worried hearts and knows more about us than we do ourselves." She can be the worry expert, but God is the expert on her. He knows her. He has not given her a spirit of fear. He has given her love and power and strength and courage to work through any worry that comes her way. He is greater. As she learns to move forward in courage, He'll strengthen her heart with each step. And I believe He'll surprise you by strengthening yours right alongside hers.

Key Points to Remember

- Avoidance strengthens anxiety. Rescuing communicates that she needs rescuing. She needs the opposite message.

- Bravery exists in the presence of fear, not the absence of it.
- Children with anxiety crave and can demand predictability. We don't want to play by the Worry Monster's rules.
- Safety behaviors and rituals strengthen the anxiety more than they strengthen your daughter.
- Anxious children believe that control will keep them safe. Rather than her learning to control the anxiety, the anxiety controls her. Her safety is contingent on her control.
- Asking continual questions can become a safety behavior for children. Your answers are not what they need . . . they need your help in learning to recognize and silence the Worry Monster's voice in the questions.
- Avoidance not only strengthens the anxiety but makes your daughter feel worse about herself in the process.
- When you make accommodations for your daughter, you encourage dependence more than independence. Accommodations strengthen her anxious symptoms and diminish her ability to work through the worry.
- You can't work harder than she does to defeat her Worry Monster.
- Girls who worry often funnel all of their emotions into the "appropriate outlet" of worry. They need our help in developing an emotional vocabulary, which is their first and most foundational tool in defeating the Worry Monster.
- Exposure therapy is a necessary part of helping your daughter learn to work through her worries, one goal at a time. She needs your support in setting and practicing goals as she builds up her confidence and bravery muscles.
- Problem solving is one of the most important tools in her fight against the Worry Monster. Girls who worry doubt their ability to solve problems on their own. Your

confidence in and questions for her will help her find her problem-solving voice.

- Her ownership and your collaboration are two of the most important tools in the fight against the Worry Monster.
- A predetermined system of rewards will create more buy-in and fun as she does the hard work of fighting the Worry Monster.
- The Worry Monster is not going to go down without a fight, and that fight, at times, may look more like her fighting against you. She needs consistency from you in those times—consistent strength and support.
- Another important weapon in your and her fight against worry is flexibility. Flexibility quiets down an overactive amygdala.

Understanding Yourself and Your Daughter Better

What has your daughter been avoiding or trying to avoid recently?

How do you see your daughter demanding predictability? Comfort?

What safety behaviors do you recognize in your daughter? Any in yourself?

How do you notice your daughter seeking control?

Does your daughter ask continual questions? How do you typically respond? How could you respond differently?

What are three ways you have been unknowingly accommodating your daughter's worries?

How have you been taking on more of the work in defeating her worries than she has?

How can you practice an emotional vocabulary more at home?

What is one goal you would like to see your daughter move toward? How can you help her set up and practice her ladder of exposures? Take the time to do it this week and note how she feels about herself in the process.

What is one problem that your daughter is facing right now? How could you help her develop more problem solving on her own?

How can you give your daughter more ownership in the process? How can you come alongside her with support and collaboration rather than your own ownership?

What are some rewards you believe would incentivize your daughter? Sit down together and come up with twenty rewards of varying points to help her buy in.

How are you doing in terms of consistency with your daughter and her worry work? What could you do differently?

How can you incorporate more flexibility into your family life?

HOPE

7. Trouble

It may sound funny to start a section on hope with the word *trouble*. But do you remember the verse we said we'd come back to in these last few chapters? John 16:33: "In this world you will have trouble." But things don't end there. The trouble we experience can lead to something good.

> We also glory in our sufferings, because we know that *suffering produces perseverance; perseverance, character; and character, hope.* And hope does not put us to shame, because God's love has been poured out into our hearts through the Holy Spirit, who has been given to us.
>
> Romans 5:3–5 (emphasis added)

It's true. Our girls will suffer and have trouble. We all will, in big and small ways. So we can and should expect trouble—not to dwell on it, but to be prepared for it, knowing that suffering produces perseverance, perseverance produces character, and character produces hope.

Science has also shown how trouble and adversity can help us. In *The Yes Brain*, Daniel Siegel and Tina Payne Bryson write about posttraumatic growth that happens for up to 70 percent of trauma survivors.[1] They report profound positive transformation as a result of coping with trauma and other challenging life circumstances. They write, "Allowing kids to face adversity, to feel disappointment and other negative emotions, and even to fail . . . [helps them] develop grit and perseverance."[2]

I learned a hard lesson about adversity and expectations more than a decade ago on a four-hundred-mile bike ride. It was a ten-day fund-raising trip for Daystar with my friends Melissa and Mimi. A gracious family had generously offered Daystar a $100,000 matching grant to help buy a little yellow house where we could counsel kids, and we were determined to raise money toward the purchase.

When I first started at Daystar in 1993, our office was in the ugliest building in Green Hills, our neighborhood in Nashville. The outside was some kind of stucco-like, gray concrete. The inside smelled like the nail salon downstairs. And the office next to ours was occupied by a pawnbroker who didn't seem completely on the up-and-up. Still, we did our best to make our office feel warm and inviting to the kids and families who walked through our doors. (Yes, it was safe, albeit a little sketchy.) The halls inside of Daystar were sunshine yellow. We had spiced tea brewing and quilts hung, and we used lamplight instead of fluorescent light. But we couldn't quite pull off the warmth we worked so hard to convey. Our hearts longed for something more.

The idea for the bike ride came up over dinner. The three of us were talking about how to raise money for the house. I'm not sure who suggested the bike ride, but Melissa and Mimi quickly jumped on the train. They thought it would be an adventure. I did not. I am not an athlete. I've never been an athlete. And I'm not very adventurous when it comes to athletic endeavors, unless they involve skis. Otherwise, I'm out. But when two of your closest friends are talking about how wonderful it's going to be . . . *"The memories will last a lifetime . . . it's for a good cause. . . ."* You get the idea. I would love to say I agreed because I felt so benevolent about Daystar. I mostly agreed because I didn't want to miss out on the fun.

A few months later, we had our bikes ready and all of the Power-Bars we could eat, and we set off. Day one, literally mile one, I had a flat tire. And it was all downhill—or uphill—from there, at least for me. At some point during every single day, I cried. It was typically around mile twenty-eight—when the end of the forty-mile daily stretch still felt far off and Melissa and Mimi were nowhere in sight.

Jumping to the end of the story, I'm happy to say we did it! The three of us raised $80,000 for Daystar, and others jumped in and raised the rest. We've now been in what one boy called "the little yellow house that helps people" for over ten years, and it truly is the house of our dreams.

Weeks after we returned from our trip, I realized what had been going on with me those ten days. Yes, I was tired. Yes, it was hard work. But more than anything, the ride didn't match my expectations. I pictured cruising along a beautiful road with two of my best friends. I pictured fall leaves and hay bales in the distance. I envisioned us laughing together and maybe singing silly songs. We had none of that. My friends were sweet—when I would finally catch up to them at the end of the day. I saw hay bales—when I could focus on something other than mile after mile that all felt uphill. And I tried to sing songs by myself, but it just wasn't the same. My expectations got in the way and were my downfall.

As a counselor to kids in this generation, their unrealistic expectations often play a part in their downfall as well.

Their Expectations

The Culture Today

"I'm not sure who told you life wasn't going to be hard." Last summer, this was one of the most memorable (and eventually hopeful) statements Melissa made to the kids at our Hopetown camp. She went on to talk about how life can be and often will be profoundly difficult. Friends will disappoint them. Their parents will disappoint them. They'll disappoint themselves. Things won't turn out like they hope or expect. There is pain, but she reminded every kid what God promises us in the midst of the pain. (More on that to come, especially in chapter 9.)

We've already talked about how, as adults who love kids, we step in and try to protect them. It's like we're trying to shield them from the trouble Jesus spoke about in John 16:33.

The attitude of many parents? *Nope, you won't have trouble, because I'm going to pull you out of it.*

A few years ago, the family of a tenth-grade girl sued the local volleyball club because they were unhappy about her limited playing time.[3] In this world, that girl won't have trouble, if her parents can do anything about it. They are telling her that life shouldn't be and isn't hard.

It's not just parents who are sending the wrong message, however. It's also the culture. Thanks to curated social media accounts, in particular, kids are being influenced by other kids who make life look easy and perfect, like they're happy and part of every birthday party or high school hangout possible. They can become "insta-famous" for the way they put on makeup or lip sync over apps, or even the way they make slime. Just flip that phone around and hit the Live button. The friends and followers will amass.

Girls today measure themselves against a Pinterest version of life, where everyone else seems to look better and live better. And be happier. And thinner. And surrounded by other happy and thin friends. They also apparently live where there's no depression or anxiety, or even sadness or worries. Actually, at great cost to girls, there seems to be a push to make anxiety and depression look cool and edgy in TV shows, movies, and other media.

Technology and the culture that it has created are changing the expectations of the girls we love. Here are just a few of the expectations I've heard from girls over the years.

> *"I will have a best friend in elementary school who wants to have sleepovers and playdates every weekend."*
> *"My best friend will never leave me out and will always include me."*
> *"I will make straight A's all through school."*

"I'll be invited to every birthday party."

"I'll find friends who make me feel accepted, loved, and safe every day at school."

"I won't get just 94s; I'll get 100s."

"I'll have the best group of friends who will stay with me from middle school up until we're bridesmaids in each other's weddings."

"I'll get my dream car, wrapped with a huge bow, when I turn sixteen."

"I'll find a boyfriend in high school who asks me to homecoming and then prom in the most romantic, creative ways ever."

"I'll meet my husband in college. We'll have kids in our late twenties, after traveling and drinking coffee in fun places. We'll be madly in love with each other every day."

"He will be perfect."

"I'll be a size 0."

And it gets worse . . .

"I'll be brave no matter what the circumstances."

"I'll be kind always and never feel frustrated with myself."

"I won't ever have conflict with anyone."

"I'll feel good about myself always."

"I'll have confidence no matter what is going on around me."

"I'll be smart and beautiful, and I'll love others well and look like nothing bothers me."

"In this world, I won't have trouble."

I'm not actually hearing all of these statements out loud, although I am hearing a few. But they reflect the expectations and the disappointment of way too many of the girls I'm counseling today.

I believe unrealistic expectations are part of the reason the rates of depression, anxiety, and even suicide are skyrocketing. A study by the Center for Disease Control and Prevention's National

Center for Health Statistics found that the rate of death from suicide has risen 30 percent since 2000. For women, in particular, suicide rates have doubled. And even more tragic, the rate of suicide among girls has grown threefold during the same period.[4]

Social media is influencing girls to have thoughts such as, *My life should look like hers. And hers and hers and hers. If it does, it's what I pictured. No gratitude needed. If it doesn't, I'm lost. I have no idea how to handle it or work through it. Something is wrong with me. My life is miserable. The problem is bigger, and I'm smaller and helpless to do anything about it.*

Our girls need us to communicate something different—something better.

The Church Today

As a writer and speaker, I follow lots of other writers and speakers on Instagram. Other than that, I only follow my closest friends, because I'm susceptible to the highlight-reel effects of social media too. I can forget that my world will have trouble when I look at other people's worlds. But honestly, I expect more from fellow travelers who are on the same road.

For years, many in the church have spoken out against the "prosperity gospel" that became popular with televangelists in the 1980s. I believe it is still very much a part of our culture today, with different voices and perspectives. The oversimplification is this: If you follow God, He'll bless you in tangible, earthly ways. Or at least in the ways you want. It used to be more about health and wealth. Today, it seems to be more about the food you eat, the places you go, and the wonderful, beautiful people who love you well in the midst of it.

Today's prosperity gospel seems to promise you'll have more friends. You'll get married at the age you plan on and have the number of children you pray for. You can have the career you believe God has called you to, make an ample living doing it, and have a social media profile about your "amazing husband and four precious children." You can start your own blog or podcast telling others—through your redemptive struggle—how to do the same, making even your tears look lovely.

I'm not trying to sound snarky, which seems to be trendy these days on social media too. God has been profoundly gracious to me and to all of us in tangible, wonderful ways. But the lives we're presenting sound a lot like the expectations of the girls we love. And as someone who has sat with thousands of people over the years behind the closed doors of confidentiality, I believe we're hurting others with this misleading presentation.

I hurt for the parents who have lost a child and are scrolling through the posts on holidays showing "perfect" families. I hurt for the estranged daughter—and mother—on Mother's Day, as she reads about so many relationships that seem to be what she wishes she had. I hurt for people who are divorcing and read anniversary posts about the perfect marriages God has blessed their friends with. I feel it on most every major holiday and lots of days in between. I know social media has become a place where we post milestones and celebrations. I do it too. But I also know plenty of marriages that are not quite what the captions convey. And I know lots of people, of all ages, who thought they were "best friends" until someone else gained the coveted title on Instagram.

I don't want to be hypocritical here. I post plenty of positive things on Instagram. But I hope and pray that I can use truth in my words, even when they're words of encouragement or praise. I try not to use words like "best" and "most" on purpose. I show fun and good things, but I also want to show the truth of what my life is and isn't—for the sake of my own sense of integrity and for girls and for vulnerable and even downright normal friends who might follow me.

Here's where I believe we miss the mark, not just on social media but in the church, in general. Our version of the prosperity gospel is not just in the pictures we post, but also in how we convey our lives. It does look like we're living in the midst of those very things the girls today expect. And even though my life has so much good in it, it sure doesn't look the way I pictured or prayed for when I was seventeen.

I recently read a quote by a Christian author I respect a great deal but who will remain nameless. He said something to the effect that contentment is when we reach the place where we are headed in life. I don't know about you, but I haven't reached where I was headed. Or at least where I thought I was headed. But I like so much of where I've reached. I believe God has called me here. And there has been so much purpose. And a lot of pain too. In this world, I have definitely had trouble. Some of that trouble sounds inspiring and looks like beauty from ashes, and some of it doesn't. I believe it will. But not yet. And I'm afraid we're doing the kids in our lives—and in our churches—a terrible disservice when we present it all in this beautiful, Pinterest-worthy package.

As believers, we often think life is a formula, that two plus two always equals four, that following Jesus equals happiness. I would love nothing more than for that to be the case. My life *has hope* because I follow Jesus. However, I don't believe that makes my life happy. Or that the happiness stays for long. I don't believe it's what Jesus promised either. Two plus two sometimes equals five. Your spouse dies unexpectedly just when you're starting a family. Your career never takes off in the way you imagined. Two kind parents don't necessarily make for a kind, easy child.

Still, I believe God never makes mistakes. There is good and life and light this side of heaven. And yes, there's also trouble. Kids, when they get to a certain age, and if they're honest, know it to be true. But they sure need us to be honest with them, or their reality and their expectations will never match up in a way that brings hope.

Their Reality

I recently joined the Daystar staff at a school on an early, sad Monday morning. A middle school boy had taken his life over the weekend, and the administration asked us to be on hand to support the students, the parents, and the faculty. We were honored to be asked and, at the same time, grieved at such an unnecessary and tragic loss for this dear community.

I sat there watching the students in the boy's grade file into the school's chapel. As they did, the middle school principal put her hands on each one of them, looked them in the eye, and said some version of "I love you," "You're not alone," or "I'm here for you." I still get teary remembering her compassionate face and the strength of her words. Then the headmaster of the school stood up to speak to the students and parents. One of the first sentences out of his mouth was "What-ifs are from Satan."

He is right. The what-ifs we've been talking about that the Worry Monster tries to throw at your daughter are from Satan, even—and maybe especially—in the case of something as devastating as losing a friend to suicide.

I can almost guarantee that every child today over the age of thirteen has either known someone in their school who has attempted suicide or at least talked about it. It's a reality for our kids. I also know entirely too many children who have lost a parent to suicide or who worry that they might. In our post-9/11 culture, children also think about terrorism and plane crashes and suicide bombers in ways we never did. They constantly hear about murders and mass shootings that cause them to have worries we never would have imagined when we were growing up.

In some ways, it seems ironic that they can be prepared for the big things that might happen and still be surprised by the little things. Or at least the more personal and inevitable things.

We're teaching kids how to hide under their desks at school in case of an intruder, but we're not teaching them how to handle a family member who disappoints them. We've got lessons upon lessons on bullying prevention, but we're not teaching them healthy conflict resolution. Maybe it's part of why the Americas have the highest levels of anxiety in the world.[5] The kids we love are getting the message that the unspeakable happens, but we're not preparing them for the daily troubles that make up life. Your girl needs to learn to function in the midst of both . . . not only to function, but to have hope.

Their Hope (and Ours)

Go back a few pages and reread the list of expectations many girls have. How many of them were fulfilled in your life? I sure hope that some of them have been. But my guess is the majority of them haven't. Or they haven't been fulfilled to the letter of the expectation. How many of those expectations have you unwittingly helped to convey to your child and others? What do you wish someone had said to you instead? Here's what I wish I had known when I was a girl of eight or eighteen.

> You will have good friends along the way, although they may not be the most popular friends.
>
> Kindness is more important than cool in a friend every time.
>
> Even the best of friends will hurt your feelings and leave you out sometimes.
>
> Learning how to handle conflict is more important than having a friendship where there isn't any.
>
> Every important relationship in your life will be hard sometimes.
>
> You won't be invited to every birthday party.
>
> Just because you're not someone's best friend doesn't mean you're not still a friend. Everyone has a closest few.
>
> People can still really love you and hurt your feelings, even at the same time.
>
> There is no perfect friend.
>
> There is no perfect guy.
>
> There is certainly no perfect teenage boy.

Every college student feels lonely, thinks they chose the wrong college, and wishes they could transfer sometimes.

There is no perfect marriage.

Every job has hard days when you wish you had chosen something else.

Parenting is hard. You will love your kids like crazy, and you will be glad when summer break is over.

Through every stage of your life, you will worry at times. You'll worry about the things and people that are most important to you, and sometimes you'll worry about things that don't even matter.

You will feel sad and angry and hurt often. Daily. But those feelings do not define you. You get to pick what defines you.

You'll never feel 100 percent confident.

You can feel courageous and fearful at the same time.

You will fail. And fail in big and little ways a million times over the course of your life.

Your failure does not define you either.

You'll often feel like something is wrong with you. You'll feel like you're the only one who _____ or who doesn't _____. You're not. And it's not.

You are exactly whom God meant for you to be, even though you won't feel like it most of the time.

In this world, you will have trouble and have it a lot.

But you can always have hope because of Jesus.

Jesus is the one friend who will never disappoint you or let you down.

Several years ago, I worked with a family whose daughter had been diagnosed with a chronic illness. They were told that this illness was going to take her life. Her tenacious family pursued every type of treatment imaginable. And now, almost fifteen years later, she's not only surviving, but she's thriving in college. When she was eight years old, however, her mom shared this poem with me that her daughter had written.

> I am a girl who believes in angels because I've been
> through tough times.
> I wonder how we can make our world a better place.
> I hear angels laughing in the distance.
> I see myself walking out on stage in my Broadway show.
> I want all children to get an education.
> I am a girl who believes in angels because I've been
> through tough times.
>
> I pretend I am a famous actress.
> I feel like I can do anything.
> I touch my soft warm blanket at night.
> I worry that I am not good enough for the world.
> I cry at the sight of a hospital bed.
> I am a girl who believes in angels because I've been
> through tough times.
>
> I understand feeling frustrated.
> I say, everything is okay in the end—if it's not okay, it's not
> the end.
> I dream I am a famous actress.
> I try to reach out and help my community.
> I hope other people can someday see me as the nice girl
> not just the sick girl.
> I am a girl who believes in angels because I've been
> through tough times.

This young girl had to let go of her expectations of the perfect life early. In fact, she traded those expectations for something much more lasting: hope. I believe her hope is a direct result of the suffering she went through. She didn't let the sufferings strengthen her worries; instead, God used those sufferings to strengthen her heart. Her expectations and her reality folded together under His care.

From all of my counseling experience and research on anxiety, I agree with this statement by David Clark and Aaron Beck, authors of *The Anxiety and Worry Workbook*: "Most worry is useless at best and counterproductive at worst."[6] It does nothing for our hearts or for the hearts of the girls we love. They will have trouble. They can learn to expect worries and even anxiety if they're smart and conscientious and lean that way. But the experts agree that worry is useless. More importantly, so does Jesus.

> Therefore I tell you, do not worry about your life, what you will eat or drink; or about your body, what you will wear. Is not life more than food, and the body more than clothes? Look at the birds of the air; they do not sow or reap or store away in barns, and yet your heavenly Father feeds them. Are you not much more valuable than they? Can any of you by worrying add a single hour to your life? . . . Therefore do not worry about tomorrow, for tomorrow will worry about itself. Each day has enough trouble of its own.
>
> Matthew 6:25–27, 34

I recently met with an eleven-year-old for her first visit to Daystar. We were talking about different feelings, and I asked which ones she felt the most. When I got to worry, she said, "I don't really worry very much." I was honestly surprised. She was the first girl in months I had talked with who didn't worry. She went on to say, "There's just no reason to. I'm reading a devotional right now that talks about worry. There are these two birds talking in a tree branch. One said to the other, 'Do you see all of those people running around down there, worrying?' 'I do,' the other bird said. 'They must not have the same Savior that we do.'"

As I have said a few times, your daughter will face trouble in her life. But that trouble truly can lead to hope, especially when she learns to live with the expectation that God will be with her in the midst of the trouble. Worry doesn't help. Hope does, through Christ.

Key Points to Remember

- Girls today have greater expectations but less hope than children in generations past.
- Girls' expectations are set not only by us as we try to protect them but also by the culture and media surrounding them.
- Unrealistic expectations are contributing to the skyrocketing rates of depression, anxiety, and even suicide.
- Our lives don't necessarily look like we thought they would when we were seventeen. Neither will your girl's, but you can help her find a real sense of hope when her expectations don't match her reality.
- What-ifs are from Satan.
- Your daughter lives in a reality where fear is a part of her everyday life.
- We're often doing a better job preparing kids for trouble on a big-picture scale than the kinds of daily troubles they're already experiencing.
- We not only need to help girls have expectations that prepare them for the trouble that is inevitable, but we also need to help them know a faith that is transformational in the midst of that trouble.
- Suffering truly does produce perseverance; perseverance, character; and character, hope. It's both biblical and scientific.
- Girls can trade their unrealistic expectations for something much more lasting: hope.
- Suffering can strengthen her worries or strengthen her heart.
- Worry doesn't help. Hope does, through Christ. She can take heart in Him right in the midst of trouble.

Understanding Yourself
and Your Daughter Better

How have you inadvertently kept your girl from experiencing the beginning of John 16:33—"In this world you will have trouble"?

How do you see your daughter's expectations impacted by her culture and social media?

What expectations do you believe she has about her life?

What kinds of messages do you believe your daughter is getting about life from the church? From you about life as a Christian? What about from your own social media posts?

What kinds of big-picture fears does your daughter live with today? How is she prepared for those? How does she feel about them?

How prepared is your daughter for personal troubles?

Read the second list of expectations. Which ones does your daughter need to hear? What would you add to the list?

How have you seen trouble impact your daughter's life for good? Have a conversation with her about suffering that eventually led to hope, and spell out each step along the way: suffering, perseverance, character, and hope. If she has a hard time seeing those elements in her experience, tell her how you've seen each in her life, as a result of trouble.

8. Take Heart

"In this world you will have trouble. But take heart! I have overcome the world."—John 16:33

In the activity book for elementary-aged girls, *Braver, Stronger, Smarter*, I write a lot about my dog, Lucy. She is adorable, I have to say. She has counseled kids every day with me for ten years. She is the epitome of the Shakespeare quote, "Though she be but little, she is fierce"[1]—a fierce eight-pound mop of a black and white and gray Havanese mix.

I named Lucy after my favorite Chronicles of Narnia character. I was inspired by one particular scene from the movie *The Chronicles of Narnia: Prince Caspian*. It's right after Lucy tells the great Lion, Aslan, "I wish I was braver." His very Aslan-ish response? "If you were any braver, you would be a lioness." The scene cuts to the entire Telmarine army on one side of a vast bridge. On the other side, Lucy steps forward alone. Out of her robes, she draws the smallest dagger of a knife—one little knife to defeat the entire Telmarine army. And then Aslan, a Christ figure, quietly and gallantly walks up beside Lucy, and it's clear she takes heart.[2]

The Greek root of the word *heart* in John 16:33 means walking out courage in boldness and confidence.[3] My little Lucy does that too. She takes on every dog of every size we ever meet, or she tries to. Lucy takes heart. Both Lucys do. And we want to teach your girl to do the same.

The great thing about taking heart is that it's not really our heart that matters. It's God's. His love gives us confident courage. When we face trouble, Aslan (God) will walk right beside us. And before us. You can have hope for your daughter's heart because of His love.

God's heart also brings with it four essential tools in her fight against her Worry Monster. Actually, they're more than tools. I'd call them cornerstones. Just as suffering leads to perseverance, which leads to character, which leads to hope, when it comes to worry, trust leads to patience, which leads to peace, which leads to gratitude. We decide to trust. We pray for patience. We make room for peace. We practice gratitude. One gives way to the other as we take heart. And these four cornerstones are enough to hold up the house that will not be shaken by worry.

Trust

Writer and theologian Henri Nouwen said, "When we worry, we have our hearts in the wrong place."[4] As I have pored over books on anxiety and worry, I have been surprised to find very little written about faith. Or, at least, very little about faith intersecting with good, practical tools to help. We need both so badly. We want our faith to inform every aspect of our lives, including, and maybe especially, our worries. We need and want practical tools to fight the Worry Monster. But we need more than tools. We need cornerstones. The most foundational cornerstone is trust.

For years, Melissa has told the kids at Hopetown, "Trust is the antidote to anxiety." Building trust is our starting point in counseling. It was what Lucy walked out onto the bridge with—trust in Aslan much more than the little knife she carried in her hand. Knives help but simply aren't enough to defeat an army of Telmarines or a Worry Monster.

In *The Message* paraphrase of the Bible, Jesus' words to one of our favorite worriers in Luke 10:41–42 are "Martha, dear Martha, you're fussing far too much and getting yourself worked up over nothing. Only one thing is essential." Of course, her sister, Mary, had chosen to sit at the feet of Jesus, to trust Him with her time and heart.

Like it was for Martha, it's easy for us to get worked up over nothing at all and forget to trust. Trust for you might mean believing that God is with your girl right now, that He will get her through the troubles she's experiencing at school or with friends. That He has given her the courage she needs to work through even the worst of her worries. Trust for her might look like stepping into her bravery even when she feels fear, remembering that God has taken care of her thus far.

Anxiety's ability to cloud memory is not only an issue of the mind but also of the heart. Your daughter will have trouble remembering how she's been brave in times past. She will also forget God's faithfulness. I'm afraid we're prone to forget too.

. . . .

In 2018, I had the honor of participating in what's known as the Jungle Pastors' Conference. It was in the middle of the Brazilian jungle on the Amazon River. If you used Google Earth to find our location, it would zoom in on trees, lots and lots of trees, until finally finding a tiny, cleared-out spot on the riverbank. Area pastors and their spouses travel for days by flat-bottomed boats and canoes to get to this conference put on by an organization I love called Justice & Mercy International.

Throughout the conference, the pastors and their spouses hear from a variety of gifted pastors, speakers, and Bible teachers. They worship and pray together and meet with a team from JMI to share about the needs of their villages and how JMI can help and pray for them. I was, needless to say, blown away not only by their stories, but by their trust. I was also blown away by how many talked about depression among the people of their villages, but not one I spoke with talked about anxiety.

Pastor after pastor told stories of the floods that take place in their villages. When they live along the river, their homes and churches are flooded and destroyed regularly. They live without homes and with little food. One pastor talked about going into his church building each Sunday with his machete to clear out the snakes so that the church members could safely enter the building. That takes a *lot* of trust in my book.

One pastor and his wife told another story. As we sat down to talk, they said that they had traveled five days by boat to come to the conference. They had four children, ranging from five years old to twenty, whom they had left at home. "We knew that God called us here . . . to learn more about how we could care for the people in our church and village," the pastor said. "We want to be the hands and feet of Jesus to them. But we had to leave our children alone to come. We didn't have any family to help. And they didn't have any food." His wife quietly interjected at that point, "But we believe God is providing for them while we are gone. In fact, I know He is right now." Her belief was not like ours. She didn't need repeated "we're fine" texts from her family to fully trust God. She had learned from experience that He takes care of His children—and hers.

This woman's words were simple, but the heart and trust behind them were not. I would venture to say that many of us in America have never experienced that kind of trust in God because we've never had to. Henri Nouwen says, "The beginning of the spiritual life is often difficult not only because the powers which cause us to worry are so strong but also because the presence of God's Spirit seems barely noticeable."[5] For this pastor and his wife, God's Spirit was profoundly noticeable. They trusted in His Spirit, His provision, and His love. They remembered His faithfulness in times past. I believe they didn't live with anxiety because of their immense trust. We live with anxiety often because of our lack of trust. It's not that we can't see His Spirit because it's barely there. It's that we don't see the Spirit because our eyes are more fixed on our worry than on our trust.

How can you help your daughter fix her eyes on something different? How can you fix yours? How can we all remember God's faithfulness in a way that grows our trust in our future? In His heart for us? Here are a few practical suggestions:

1. *Build your own "family Ebenezer."* Create a place where you can build a monument, of sorts, with small stones, referencing 1 Samuel 7:12, where "Samuel took a stone and set it between Mizpah and Shen. . . . Saying, 'Thus far the LORD has helped us.'" Once a month, or every so often, go back to that monument and lay new stones to remember God's faithfulness in certain instances, naming them out loud together.

2. *Tell stories of trust.* Teach your children about Abraham and various people in the Bible who trusted God. Talk about the stories, asking your daughter to imagine herself as a participant. What would she have felt? What does she think that person was feeling? Why would they be willing to trust God in that moment? How did trust change things for them?

3. *Read books and sing songs about trust.* The Jesus Storybook Bible by Sally Lloyd-Jones, *Jesus Calling: 365 Devotions for Kids* by Sarah Young, and *Love Does for Kids* by Bob Goff and Lindsey Goff Viducich are all books that can serve as reminders of God's faithfulness in times of trouble. Listen to Ellie Holcomb's children's album, *Sing*. Rain for Roots has several albums as well—and each has specific songs that reference trust in the case of worry. For older kids, worship music can be an incredible teacher and reminder of God's faithfulness and nearness to them. A girl I counsel right now lost a parent, and she practices calligraphy with the lyrics to worship songs, just to remind herself of their meaning when she feels sad or anxious.

4. *Reference trust in daily conversation about your own life.*
Comments like "I'm having a hard time with _____, but
I trust that God is taking care of me" can serve as a reminder of the foundational importance of trust. Talk like
you remember His faithfulness as well. Go back to times
in the past when He has provided for you and shown you
His love.

5. *Model what trust looks like as it relates to your own worry.*
We can't ask kids to go anywhere we're not willing to go
ourselves. If your kids looked to you as a model of what
it looks like to trust God with the things they're worried
about, what would they see? What do you want to do
differently?

We continue to shout our praise even when we're hemmed in
with troubles, because we know how troubles can develop passionate patience in us, and how that patience in turn forges the
tempered steel of virtue, keeping us alert for whatever God will
do next. In alert expectancy such as this, we're never left feeling
shortchanged. Quite the contrary—we can't round up enough con-
tainers to hold everything God generously pours into our lives
through the Holy Spirit!

Romans 5:3–5, The Message

"We continue to shout our praise even when we're hemmed in
with troubles" sounds a lot like trust to me. Trust, in this sense,
is the antidote to anxiety. We can't be anxious and trust at the
same time. We trust when we remember God's faithfulness. We
trust when we believe that His faithfulness not only impacted our
past but impacts our future as well. No need for worry in either
case. We trust because we know how troubles develop passionate
patience in us.

Your daughter needs you to remember examples of God's faithfulness in her life and yours. She needs you to act as her memory
when she forgets and to remind her. And she needs you to live out

of that trust in passionate patience as you wait for all that God is generously pouring into both of your lives.

Patience

"Above all, trust in the slow work of God."

A poem I recently came across begins with these words.[6] How's your trust in the slow work of God going these days? I think the slow part is honestly what keeps me from trusting most of the time. God's work is slow—too slow many days, by my timing. My pastor and friend, Danny, talks about how the speed of God is more like five miles per hour, while we're living at fifty. Five miles per hour takes a looong time to get anywhere. But you sure see more in the process.

Yes, God's work is slow. Patience helps us slow down and trust in that work. Worry, on the other hand, speeds everything up. Our body kicks into high gear with our sympathetic nervous system. Our minds rev up and our thoughts spin in the one-loop roller coaster. And our hearts, then, race ahead of God. In the process, we stop taking heart. We stop trusting. The questions, in turn, move from "What if . . . ?" to "Why has He not . . . ?" The answer is sometimes that He just hasn't yet.

As I'm sure you've heard, *fear not* is one of the most used phrases in the Bible. Another is simply the word *wait*. From the New Testament to the Old, *wait* brings with it lots of meanings.

The Hebrew words for *wait* (and there are quite a few) communicate messages such as "to bind together," "to look patiently," "tarry," "hope, expect, look eagerly," "rest," "be still," "accept," "receive."[7]

Psalm 130:5–6 says, "I wait for the Lord, my soul does wait, and in His word do I hope. My soul waits for the Lord more than the watchmen for the morning; indeed, more than the watchmen for the morning" (nasb).

In Old Testament times, the watchman had to keep an eye on the city, or on the flocks, until morning. And while I would imagine the morning sometimes was a long time in coming, it always came. He waited with patience and with trust in the sun.

Waiting always involves the passage of time.

Your daughter's wars against her worry are going to require patience. It is going to take time to build both her voice and her courage. We talked before about allowing your daughter to stay in the anxiety-provoking situation for fifteen to twenty minutes, until the initial feelings of fear pass. Those little moments will require patience on her part. But she'll need patience in the bigger sense as well. The entire process of fighting her Worry Monster will feel like waiting for the sun to rise at times.

It's likely already felt too long for you, as a grown-up who loves her. You want her to feel better, to not feel hindered by her anxiety. She wants the same thing. She'll get there. Patience, not only in the process but in God as He grows her strength, is one of the most important parts of her learning what it means to take heart.

Waiting involves confident expectation.

As Psalm 27:14 says, "Wait on the LORD; be of good courage, and He shall strengthen your heart; Wait, I say, on the LORD!" (NKJV).

The sun always rises. Waiting involves the confident expectation that God is able to do immeasurably more than she can ask or imagine, according to His power that is at work in her (Ephesians 3:20). She needs reminders of that power and that God is at work in her waiting. She's probably not going to see it or feel it. She hasn't yet had the life experiences that can teach us to believe with that kind of confidence. She's your watchman in training. She needs you to take her on the hill with you, reminding her that the morning will come . . . that the sounds aren't those of intruders but of crickets. She needs to sit with you as you strain your eyes together to watch for the first glimmers of dawn. She needs you to wait with and sometimes for her when the night feels long. God is strengthening her heart in the process, and enlarging so much more in her.

Waiting brings growth.

Have I said that waiting is hard for me? I'm not a patient person. I don't think many of us type A folks are. We make things happen, rather than wait for them to happen. Maybe that's why Romans 8 is one of my all-time favorite chapters in the Bible, particularly the part that talks about being enlarged in the waiting.

> That is why waiting does not diminish us, any more than waiting diminishes a pregnant mother. We are enlarged in the waiting. We, of course, don't see what is enlarging us. But the longer we wait, the larger we become, and the more joyful our expectancy. Meanwhile, the moment we get tired in the waiting, God's Spirit is right alongside helping us along.
>
> Romans 8:24–26 THE MESSAGE

When we worry, we live in the immediate. We want comfort and security, and we want it right now. This passage reminds us that when we wait, good things come. God is enlarging your daughter in the waiting. He's enlarging you too. He is growing her strength as she has patience. He is making her braver and stronger and smarter. She, again, doesn't yet know that to be true. All she knows is that she is still hearing the Worry Monster's voice . . . she's still fighting . . . she is not yet who she wants to be. She needs your help and your reminders.

1. *Grow something together.* Plant a tree, or even a flower bulb. Watch it. Talk about it regularly. Remind her that God is doing something with that seed to grow it into much more than it currently is.
2. *Talk often about things you believe God is growing in her.* Point them out to her. Ask her what she believes He might be growing too.
3. *Give her things to look forward to.* I met with a little girl today who has to wait until she's twelve to get her ears

pierced. What is your daughter waiting on? Waiting grows the muscle of patience and helps her learn that good things happen in the midst of the waiting.

4. *Do a driving experiment.* Drive down a quiet street at the speed limit. Ask her what she notices. Drive down the same street much more slowly. What does she see now that she didn't see before? Talk about how slowing down helps us see more things in life.

5. *Talk about something you're each waiting expectantly for.*

Peace

As I was researching worry, one of the things I read about was the importance of being a "nonanxious presence" in your child's life.[8] Here are Stixrud and Johnson's guidelines for being a nonanxious presence:

1. Make enjoying your kids your top parenting priority.
2. Don't fear the future.
3. Commit to your own stress management.
4. Make peace with your worst fears.
5. Adopt an attitude of nonjudgmental acceptance.[9]

I believe every one of these ideas is good and important—and next to impossible without faith. How do we make peace with our own worst fears without trust? How do we keep from fearing the future? It reminds me of the Serenity Prayer, which starts with "God, grant me the serenity to accept the things I cannot change; courage to change the things I can; and wisdom to know the difference."[10] God, grant me _____, because I sure can't do it on my own. Neither can you. And neither can she.

Clark and Beck observe, "People with anxiety problems believe that the best defense against the worst thing happening is to take control."[11] The worry experts say that the best defense is acceptance. How do we help her, and how do we move ourselves from control to acceptance? I believe the answer lies in the third cornerstone: peace. God's peace, not ours.

Philippians 4:6–7 says, "Do not be anxious about anything, but in every situation, by prayer and petition, with thanksgiving, present your requests to God. And the peace of God, which transcends all understanding, will guard your hearts and your minds in Christ Jesus." My favorite author, Frederick Buechner, puts it this way:

> "In everything," Paul says, [the Phillippians] are to keep on praying. Come Hell or high water, they are to keep on asking, keep on thanking, above all keep on making themselves known. He does not promise them that as a result they will be delivered from the worst things any more than Jesus himself was delivered from them. What he promises them instead is that "the peace of God, which passes all understanding, will keep your hearts and your minds in Christ Jesus."[12]

It is possible to make peace with your own worst fears. It's possible to help her make peace with hers. That's what the second section of this book is all about. But it's our faith that makes those things possible. Trust and patience will lead the way. And then we pray for peace. God will grant it, in time. He will bring peace in the midst of your daughter's trouble and in the midst of your trusting, nonanxious presence with her.

1. *Practice peace.* When we teach parenting seminars on raising boys and girls, my friend David Thomas talks about the importance of a neutral space for boys. He asserts that boys, in particular, have so much physicality to their emotions that they need a physical space where they can release those emotions in a constructive way. Some girls emote with that kind of physicality as well. I believe it is important for girls (and boys) to have a place where they can process, where they can draw or journal. One of my favorite suggestions is to have them stomp on bubble wrap.

But every one of us needs places to practice coping skills, to help us come down from our angry and anxious times. A young girl I see for counseling currently calls her space "The Peace Place." We all need them, and we all need to practice peace when we're feeling worried and anything but peaceful.

2. *Pray the Serenity Prayer regularly.* Let it be a conversation you have around the dinner table. What things can you change? What things can you not? What can you let go of, and how would your life look different as a result? Practice together and report back.

3. *Create quiet.* I recently started spiritual direction for the first time. If you're not familiar with it, the definition of spiritual direction, according to author David Benner, is "a prayer process in which a person seeking help in cultivating a deeper personal relationship with God meets with another for prayer and conversation that is focused on increasing awareness of God in the midst of life experiences and facilitating surrender to God's will."[13] It sounds complicated. It basically involves sitting with someone you trust who is trained in spiritual direction, praying, talking, and being quiet. It's one of the most peaceful things I've ever done. Maybe it's because I'm an introvert, but I believe we, as adults, have lost touch with a sense of quietude and peace. And kids undoubtedly have. Peace often begins in thoughtful silence. We want to encourage the girls we love to have quiet, and we need to be going to those quiet places with them. If you have a younger child, *My First Message* by Eugene Peterson is a fantastic resource for teaching children to read Scripture thoughtfully and reflectively. What does it look like for your family to literally have quiet time together? To listen in the silence? Sit outside on a Sunday afternoon with your Bible. Read and then look up at the clouds. Have an hour where you take books on the

porch. No screens. No noise. Just quiet and peace. It takes intentionality and it takes practice. We have to make room.

4. *Remember to breathe.* Breathing is important when your daughter's brain has been hijacked by the amygdala. But she also needs to practice intentional breathing when her brain is functioning normally. Breathing regularly can reset and quiet down a hypersensitive amygdala. It can also slow down her sympathetic nervous system, which is used to running on full speed. Breathing just slows her down in general. It helps her gain perspective and takes her back to a more peaceful place and the peace of God, which transcends all understanding and guards her (and your) heart and mind in Christ Jesus.

Gratitude

According to a multitude of studies, gratitude is good for our bodies, brains, and hearts. It's good for the girls in your life too. Amy Morin, a psychotherapist and author, surveyed several studies to find these important effects of gratitude:

1. **Gratitude creates opportunity for more relationships.** Even something as simple as saying "thank you" to a new friend makes them more likely to seek out a deeper friendship.

2. **Gratitude increases physical health.** Grateful people not only report fewer "aches and pains," but actually say that they feel better physically than others.

3. **Gratitude strengthens psychological health.** Gratitude lessens what we would consider more negative emotions, such as regret, frustration, jealousy, and resentment and has been proven to increase happiness and reduce depression.

4. **Gratitude develops empathy and diminishes aggression.**

5. Grateful people have better sleep habits.
6. Gratitude boosts self-confidence.
7. Gratitude grows psychological strength. . . . and also may help overcome trauma.[14]

In addition, Tamar Chanksy writes that gratitude lowers anxiety and stress.[15] Gratitude is good for us all, physically, psychologically, and relationally. It's also good for us spiritually.

Years ago, a pastor told me something I'll never forget. It's become a part of our vernacular at Hopetown and starts off many of our worship meetings at night: "Satan can't live in a thankful heart." Neither can worry, I might add. It's a little like the principle of competing demands and how worry and feeling relaxed can't coexist. When we're thankful, we can't also be anxious.

Just this past week, I met with a high school girl, who happens to be a gifted singer-songwriter (yes, I live in Nashville). As we talked, she mentioned that all of the songs she writes have what is called a "wow," pronounced "vav." She went on to explain to me that *wow* is a Hebrew letter that appears in the last few lines of many of the psalms, providing what is referred to as a "hook." She said she tries to format her music like those psalms, expressing sadness and then lament, and then turning (or hooking) back toward gratitude and hope every single time . . . thus, the wow. I immediately wanted her to share the wow with the girls in her counseling group. Not sure about you, but I could use a little more wow regularly. (For more of an illustration for psalms with wow, read Psalms 6, 13, 22, and 43.)

That night in group, as this girl shared profound truth from her life, along with a song, each of the girls talked sadness, hurts, or worries. And each ended with a wow, something she was grateful for in the midst of the emotion. Satan can't live in their thankful hearts. And gratitude turns them away from the anxiety. Gratitude turns them toward, in fact, the Giver of the good gift for which they're grateful.

1. *Write your own "wow."* Have each member of your family write a psalm to God, complete with all of the worries or sadness they're experiencing right now, and end it in a wow. Have them share at least one thing at the end for which they're thankful, and why.

2. *Start a thankful journal.* This one can be done with your entire family too. Several times a week, each person can write ten things they're thankful for in their journal as a practice. You can share them with each other regularly, if you all collectively choose to do so.

3. *Have a gratitude jar.* Keep a glass jar out in the kitchen with paper and a pen nearby. Practice randomly writing things you're grateful for on the paper anonymously, and read them periodically over dinner—not just at Thanksgiving.

4. *Have each family member create a gratitude album on their phones.* David started doing this with some of the adolescent boys he counsels. Younger kids can create gratitude albums on tablets. In the album, they place photos of people and things they love—photos that will bring them comfort and joy when they're struggling. Then, when they start to worry, they can go back to their gratitude album and flip through photos to shift their thinking away from their worries and back to a place of gratitude.

We worry. Your daughter worries. In this world, there will be trouble. But there is always hope. There is always a wow. We are called to take heart in the midst of our worry. We start with trust, move toward patience, experience peace, and end in gratitude. It's what taking heart looks like. In fact, it's what taking His heart into the places of fear looks like. God has not given us a heart of stone, but a heart of flesh. Of hope. And of courage. He has overcome the world. And in that, there is much to be grateful for.

Key Points to Remember

- In the midst of trouble, God calls us to take heart. Taking heart means exercising bold and confident courage, and it involves four cornerstones: trust, patience, peace, and gratitude.
- Trust is the antidote to worry. We learn to trust by experience. She stops trusting when she forgets God's faithfulness to her in the past. She needs you not only to remember but to be her memory. None of us can be anxious and trust at the same time.
- God's work is slow. As we wait with patience, our bodies, minds, and hearts slow down, and we're better able to see and hear His Spirit. And we're also better able to trust.
- Waiting involves the passage of time and confident expectation, and it always brings growth. Good things come in the waiting.
- Peace comes as she learns (and we do too) to move from control to acceptance. Peace is God's to grant and ours to practice.
- Gratitude is good for us and for our bodies, minds, and hearts. It also diminishes anxiety.
- Satan can't live in our thankful hearts.
- Start with trust, move toward patience, experience peace, and end in gratitude as you learn what it means to take heart.

Understanding Yourself
and Your Daughter Better

How do you want faith to impact your worry? Her worry?
How is it doing so now?

How have you seen God's faithfulness in her life in the past?
How has she?

What is something that is creating more patience in you right
now? That you're waiting on God to do?

How have you seen growth in her waiting?

When is the last time you remember peace in your home?
What about in your daughter? What would it look like to
pray for and incorporate more peace into your daily lives?

How do you notice gratitude affecting your life? Hers? What
are five things you're each grateful for right now?

How can you each take heart into the places of trouble in
your life today?

9. Overcomer

Sometimes, when girls worry, I have them choose a fight song. They can listen to the song when they're on the way to a birthday party, to take a test, or to do anything they feel worried about. Girls have chosen songs like "Brave" by Sara Bareilles, "Roar" by Katy Perry, and, one of my personal favorites, "Overcomer" by Mandisa.

So here we are. Final chapter. Final round. Your girl is learning what it means to be an overcomer of that mean old Worry Monster. She's made it this far, which means you're an overcomer too. Throughout this fight, she needs you to speak truth to her. In fact, just last night, as I was beginning this last chapter, I asked high school girls what makes them feel bravest. Their answers were as follows:

"When people I love remind me of good things I've done."

"When I get out of my comfort zone and get involved in more things."

"When I'm around people who make me feel good, like my family."

"When I do something brave, like trying out for a play."

"When I read my Bible."

"When I talk to God or my parents."

"When someone I trust reminds me it's not going to stay like this forever."

"When I remember that I don't have to be perfect, and I just try."

"When I remember not to make it about me."

"When I do the thing that I'm worried about doing."

"When people who love me remind me that I can."

"When my parents and friends notice how hard I'm trying."

"When my mom or dad tells me I'm doing a good job."

"When my parents listen and try to understand how I feel."

So many of their answers have to do with you. Especially when you listen, encourage them, and remind them of the truth of who they are.

Here is the truth about your girl.

She is brave, because God has given her courage.

> Be strong and of good courage, do not fear nor be afraid of them; for the LORD your God, He is the One who goes with you. He will not leave you nor forsake you.
>
> Deuteronomy 31:6 NKJV

> On the day I called, You answered me; You made me bold with strength in my soul.
>
> Psalm 138:3 NASB

> He is not afraid of bad news; his heart is firm, trusting in the LORD. His heart is steady; he will not be afraid.
>
> Psalm 112:7–8 ESV

> So we can confidently say, "The Lord is my helper; I will not fear; what can man do to me?"
>
> Hebrews 13:6 ESV

And this passage feels particularly poignant in light of the work your daughter has been doing:

> David also said to Solomon his son, "Be strong and courageous, and do the work. Do not be afraid or discouraged, for the LORD God, my God, is with you. He will not fail you or forsake you until all the work for the service of the temple of the LORD [or the fight against the Worry Monster] is finished."
>
> 1 Chronicles 28:20

She is strong, because God has given her His strength.

> God is our refuge and strength, an ever-present help in trouble. Therefore we will not fear, though the earth give way and the mountains fall into the heart of the sea, though its waters roar and foam and the mountains quake with their surging.
>
> Psalm 46:1–3

> So do not fear, for I am with you; do not be dismayed, for I am your God. I will strengthen you and help you; I will uphold you with my righteous right hand.
>
> Isaiah 41:10

> The LORD is my strength and my song; he has given me victory.
>
> Exodus 15:2 NLT

> The LORD is my light and my salvation—whom shall I fear? The LORD is the stronghold of my life—of whom shall I be afraid? When the wicked [or Worry Monsters] advance against me to devour me, it is my enemies and my foes who will stumble and fall. Though an army besiege me, my heart will not fear.
>
> Psalm 27:1–3

> I can do everything through Christ, who gives me strength.
>
> Philippians 4:13 NLT

She is smart, because God has given her wisdom.

For God gave us a spirit not of fear but of power and love and self-control.

2 Timothy 1:7 ESV

For the LORD gives wisdom; from his mouth come knowledge and understanding.

Proverbs 2:6

And He will be the stability of your times, a wealth of salvation, wisdom and knowledge.

Isaiah 33:6 NASB

For wisdom will enter your heart, and knowledge will be pleasant to your soul.

Proverbs 2:10

And he has filled him with the Spirit of God, with wisdom, with understanding, with knowledge.

Exodus 35:31

To you, O God of my fathers, I give thanks and praise, for you have given me wisdom and might, and have now made known to me what we asked of you.

Daniel 2:23 ESV

She is more loved than she knows. By you. By God.

There is no fear in love. But perfect love drives out fear.

1 John 4:18

The Spirit you received does not make you slaves, so that you live in fear again; rather, the Spirit you received brought about your adoption to sonship. And by him we cry, "Abba, Father."

Romans 8:15

See what great love the Father has lavished on us, that we should be called children of God! And that is what we are!

1 John 3:1

The LORD appeared to us in the past, saying: "I have loved you with an everlasting love; I have drawn you with unfailing kindness."

Jeremiah 31:3

[Love] always protects, always trusts, always hopes, always perseveres. Love never fails.

1 Corinthians 13:7–8

Do you think anyone is going to be able to drive a wedge between us and Christ's love for us? There is no way! Not trouble, . . . not backstabbing, not even the worst sins listed in Scripture. . . . None of this fazes us because Jesus loves us. I'm absolutely convinced that nothing—nothing living or dead, angelic or demonic, today or tomorrow, high or low, thinkable or unthinkable—absolutely *nothing* can get between us and God's love because of the way that Jesus our Master has embraced us.

Romans 8:35–39 THE MESSAGE

She can rest on God's promises.

The LORD will fight for you; you need only to be still.

Exodus 14:14

I want to go back to Melissa's words from chapter 7: "I'm not sure who told you life wasn't going to be hard."

If you wondered where she went with that talk, it was one of my favorites in the history of Hopetown. I want to share the rest of it with you so that you can share it with the girl you love. Or, at least, you can share the impact of God's promises with her.

Melissa went on to tell the kids, "You are going to have pain. There is light and dark, inside and outside of you. But there is a promise. God's going to keep you safe. He's going to give you a banquet, a new name, a place in the victory parade, and a permanent position of honor and a seat alongside Jesus at the head table. There is always a promise."

There is pain, but there is always a promise. It's what we live by in this world of trouble. It's why and how we take heart and have hope. It's why and how she can do the same. She will have trouble, but He has overcome the world.

Anne Lamott says, "People say you can't have faith and fear at the same time. But you can. I'm exhibit A. I prefer to think, Courage is fear that has said its prayers."[1]

Not only is courage fear that has said its prayers, but courage knows its prayers have already been answered—whether or not it can see the answer yet. I'm concerned about the messages some people are hearing about anxiety. David Clark and Aaron Beck say, "The problem with worry is that it's always about future events, and no one can know the future. So the desire for safety and certainty is futile."[2]

I don't believe this is true. There is safety and certainty because of God's promises. We know who knows the future. In fact, we don't just know who. We know Him. And He will fight for us. He already has.

. . . .

This past summer, we made up a word with our fifth- and sixth-graders. Actually, Melissa came up with it: God-fidence. We were talking about self-confidence and the fact that none of us really has much of it. *The Message* paraphrases 1 Corinthians 10:12 as, "You could fall flat on your face as easily as anyone else." (Sounds a lot like "In this world you will have trouble," doesn't it?) The verse continues: "Forget about self-confidence; it's useless. Cultivate God-confidence."

Or God-fidence.

We can have God-fidence in Him—in our futures—because of Him. Your daughter can have God-fidence in her fight against the Worry Monster. Anxiety does not have the power to define her. God will and has already fought for her. She can do the work with her tools. But He is the cornerstone of a house that cannot be shaken by worry. She can do all things through Christ who strengthens her (Philippians 4:13). He has overcome the world and every Worry Monster that's ever been or ever will be. And that is precisely why all of us can take heart. You right alongside her. There is always a promise. And there is always hope. She can do it. And so can you.

Key Points to Remember

- Girls feel bravest when someone they love reminds them of the truth of who they are.
- She is an overcomer because He has overcome the world.
- She is brave, smart, strong, and more loved than she knows. And there is plenty of Scripture to back that up.
- She can also rest on His promises. There is trouble. But there is always a promise.
- Courage is fear that has said its prayers and knows those prayers have been answered.
- Christ has overcome the world and every Worry Monster that's ever been. There is always hope.

Understanding Yourself and Your Daughter Better

What truths can you remind your girl of today? How can you encourage her?

Which of these verses do you believe she most needs to hear?

What promises do you want her to remember?

How can you remind her today that Jesus has overcome the world and her Worry Monster too?

How could you all incorporate a little more God-fidence into your lives?

Appendix 1:
Types of Anxiety

The following is a list of the most common types of anxiety that occur in children and adolescents. As Dr. Tamar Chansky points out, it bears mentioning that "the consensus across numerous studies is that the majority of anxious children have more than one anxiety disorder at a time,"[1] so you may see your daughter in more than one of the areas listed below. Please note, however, that children are not given a diagnosis based solely on the presence of symptoms but on the duration and prevalence of the symptoms and the degree of disruption those symptoms are causing.

If your daughter's home life, school life, or relationships have been negatively impacted by any of the following, I would recommend consulting with a mental health professional, particularly if the symptoms are still present after you and she have used the tools in this book. This list is not exhaustive. For further information and help, I recommend Dr. Chansky's worrywisekids.org as well as the Anxiety and Depression Association of America's adaa.org.

Generalized Anxiety Disorder (GAD) is characterized by looping worry that occurs almost constantly, and is not brought on by any specific issue or situation. Worries are connected to a variety of topics that follow your girl's development and can include any type of issue, such as danger, storms, what others think, grades, punctuality, and many more. Children with GAD catastrophize situations, live with a pervasive sense of anxiety, shy away from risks, struggle with problem solving, and lean toward perfectionism. A child who suffers from GAD, in essence, worries about worry and abhors uncertainty. Children who are diagnosed with GAD are apprehensive about the past, present, and/or the future. They struggle with concentrating, sleeping, irritability, muscle tension, restlessness, and fatigue.

Obsessive-compulsive disorder plagues more than one million children in the United States.[2] OCD has two primary components: obsessions and compulsions. Obsessions are persistent thoughts, impulses, or images that cause considerable distress and are difficult to control. Obsessions are often not related to real-life issues. Compulsions are the behaviors that a child develops to bring relief, confidence, and make the distress go away. Compulsions include checking and rechecking (homework or even their hair in the mirror), hand washing, tapping on one side of the body and then the other, counting, apologizing, and others. Bedtime rituals can also be a part of a child's compulsions, such as having a certain order of activities or a specific thing a parent has to say every night before bed. Children with obsessive-compulsive disorder can become hyper-focused on concerns such as numbers that they label as "good" or "bad," good and bad thoughts, or germs. These children are often both likable and successful, as they can manage the OCD symptoms most places outside of home and their families.

With OCD, in particular, early intervention is crucial. Exposure therapy is one of the most effective treatments with OCD (the stepladders we talked about in chapter 6). OCD is considered what many refer to as a brain glitch, not in the amygdala as in the other anxiety disorders but in the caudate nucleus. The caudate nucleus is the brain's filtering center that classifies thoughts into levels of importance or appropriateness. A caudate nucleus that is not working properly sorts all messages into the highest priority. Chanksy writes that one-third of all OCD diagnoses are a result of PANS (Pediatric Autoimmune Neuropsychiatric Disorders Associated with Streptococcal Infections). PANS used to be known as PANDAS, and emerges overnight.[3] If your child has OCD-related symptoms that occur overnight as a result of strep, consult your pediatrician immediately.

Panic Disorder is where the amygdala of the brain stays in the on position constantly. It's characterized by intense periods of anxiety that happen without warning. Children with panic disorder have symptoms much like panic attacks: sweating, difficulty breathing, feeling as if everything is closing in, and feeling like they are floating outside of themselves. Panic attacks usually last between five and twenty minutes. After panic attacks, children often end up with looping thoughts about the next panic attack— wondering when and how it will strike—and spend a great deal of time and energy trying to prevent it. As a result, they hyper-focus on any symptom that might appear to be another attack, believing they might throw up, or even die in some situations. Panic attacks often feel, especially to children, like they come on without a trigger but are actually a result of a situation that triggers the panic. One of the first steps with panic disorder is to help the child identify the trigger, and then immediately start practicing deep breathing and mindfulness skills, and then boss back the worries.

Post-Traumatic Stress Disorder (PTSD) is often the result of a hyperreactive amygdala. With PTSD, a child will reexperience a traumatic life-threatening event (or an event that was perceived as such). As a result, the child becomes fearful, agitated, and feels helpless. Symptoms of PTSD involve regressive behavior such as baby talk, clinginess to a trusted adult, or ADHD-types of behavior, such as irritability or acting out. Kids who suffer from PTSD are also hypervigilant and have sleep disturbances and flashbacks of the traumatic event. As adults who love them, our response is one of the predominant factors of how trauma will impact a child. It's of the utmost importance that we normalize their feelings and responses, create a safe place, and maintain predictable routines as much as possible.

Selective Mutism occurs when a child is unable to speak in certain situations or locations. Children with selective mutism often don't say a word outside of their homes but feel free to talk (and make up for lost time, their siblings tell me) at home. Many parents are surprised at parent–teacher conferences that a child is not talking at school. In fact, most children develop selective mutism around five years of age, when a child typically begins school. With a child dealing with selective mutism, it is important not to put too much pressure on the child, but to create a system of rewards that work toward more conversation outside of home.

Separation Anxiety Disorder is a child's intense worry about being away from one or both parents. The child fears the parent will be hurt or even die when away from them. Preschool age is the time when separation anxiety occurs the most, but it can also exist in school-aged children and even teenagers after a traumatic event. Separation from a parent is good for children. All children need to learn to self-soothe and handle discomfort. With children who struggle with separation anxiety, it's important to separate in small increments, role-play good-byes, and then work toward longer and farther separation on their ladders of exposure.

Social Anxiety Disorder is also known as social phobia. More than just shyness, social anxiety disorder can be a disabling fear of social situations. Social anxiety impacts as many as 5 percent of children.[4] Children with social anxiety are fearful of embarrassment in front of both adults and peers, which can impact not just their social lives but their academic lives, as well. They don't want to raise their hands in class or interact with adults or authority figures. Many children with social anxiety sabotage themselves, with worry distorting their perception. They monitor themselves constantly and interpret most feedback as negative, with their amygdalae driving much of their perception. As a result, children with social anxiety engage in behaviors that perpetuate the problem, either avoiding situations that might cause embarrassment (or strengthen social bonds) or drawing more attention to themselves as a form of sabotage. Children with social anxiety need to practice small steps: eye contact, ordering at a restaurant, smiling, reporting something to the teacher from her weekend. Role play is a profoundly helpful tool with children who suffer from social anxiety.

Specific Phobias are exactly as they sound—related to one specific situation, event, or object. A child who suffers from specific phobia functions relatively well until they encounter that phobia. They're unaware that the fear is irrational, and need both mindfulness activities and ladders of exposure to work through the fear. Examples of common phobias for children include vomiting, airplanes, bugs, the dark, or heights.

Trichotillomania/Tic Disorder/Tourette Syndrome are all related to and often co-occur with anxiety disorders. Trichotillomania is compulsive hair pulling. Many kids pull their hair in a certain area on their scalp, or pull out their eyebrows or eyelashes. They don't feel "right" until they pull, according to the children who suffer from this disorder.

Tic disorders are related to Tourette syndrome and can often be seen, at first, as a nervous habit. With a tic disorder, a child displays repetitive and sudden muscle movements, such as eye blinking, moving their mouth in a certain way, or making repetitive noises. Tics can be motor or verbal in nature. According to Dr. Chansky, approximately 24 percent of children experience some type of motor tic throughout their development, most minor.[5]

It's best to seek help when a child can't stop when the tic is pointed out, if the tic interferes with her daily life, or if she gets angry at herself because of the tic. The most prevalent treatment for tic disorder is habit reversal training, which teaches kids to do something other than the tic. For example, a child who makes noises can learn to swallow softly or breathe deeply instead. It can also help a child to have a place where they know they can tic freely, without judgment. Tics that develop overnight are also often a result of PANS and should be treated first by your pediatrician. Sixty percent of tics get better over time, and only 1 percent or fewer people end up with a chronic tic disorder.[6] If you are worried about your child, don't draw negative attention to the behavior. Respond first with compassion, and then brainstorm strategies to help them with habit reversal.

Tourette syndrome, says the CDC, occurs when a person has two or more motor tics and at least one vocal tic, although the tics might not always occur at the same moment.[7] Children with Tourette syndrome have shown symptoms for at least one year, and say their bodies engage in the behavior because it makes them feel safe.

Attention-Deficit/Hyperactivity Disorder (ADHD) and anxiety often occur together. They also are very similar symptomatically. Both include restlessness, distractibility, impulsivity, hyperactivity, and often agitation. Kids with ADHD, however, are distracted by things in which they're interested. Children with anxiety are distracted by fearful thoughts, looping worry, danger, and worst-case scenarios. Because ADHD medications often increase anxiety and its symptoms, it's important to have a professional help determine the more significant underlying cause.

Sensory Processing Dysfunction is what is often happening when a child is highly irritated by tags in clothing and seams in socks. They prefer leggings and dresses, and often have meltdowns over clothing choices. Food choices can also be greatly limited for children with sensory issues because of the consistency of certain foods. Many children with SPD display anxiety-related behaviors as a result of their sensory dysregulation. It's as if they can't turn down the volume on different tactile or sensory stimuli, and their emotions become out of control, as a result. We will often refer a child who struggles with sensory issues to occupational therapy first, before treating their anxiety. Helping them learn to process sensory information in a more integrated way can often reduce and even eliminate the anxiety completely.

Appendix 2: Beating the Bedtime Blues

When I ask girls when they feel most anxious, the most common answer is bedtime. When your girl is lying in bed, her mind has time to wander. The Worry Monster takes advantage and steps into the void with his loud, repetitive, alarmist voice. He brings up the past, the future, basically anything he can use to get her on the one-loop roller coaster.

Helping children sleep involves two primary components:

1. helping the child relax and
2. helping the parent cope.

In my counseling experience, both can be equally difficult. Parents often abdicate and end up falling asleep themselves in their child's bedroom, simply as a result of exhaustion. They can be masters at wearing you down when their Worry Monsters are working them over. So here are a few basic guidelines to keep in mind:

1. Let her fall asleep on her own. All children need to learn self-soothing techniques. Statistically, children whose

parents are present when the children fall asleep wake up more often during the night than those who fall asleep alone, says Chansky.[1] ·

2. Give her enough time to wind down. She needs time post-homework and post-activity to calm her brain. She can read or color or listen to music, but she needs some type of activity to help her settle and help her brain to slow back down from a busy day.

3. Help her plan for normal nighttime fears. She can have a stack of things to do when she gets fearful. She can read her book or say a Bible verse out loud. She can practice the three-doors relaxation activity (explained in chapter 4). She can count sheep or practice progressive muscle relaxation or any type of mindfulness activity.

4. Maintain a healthy mind platter. She needs adequate exercise and good nutrition to prime her for adequate sleep.

5. Make bedtime a positive experience. Don't use going to bed earlier as a consequence. Incentivize her with rewards when she either goes to bed without complaining or delaying or doesn't come out of her room after bedtime.

6. Focus on helping her get ready for sleep, not a specific time she has to fall asleep. The act of falling asleep is beyond any of our control and can easily translate into pressure for her.

7. Have her sleep in her bed. Most experts advocate that children should always sleep in their own beds. On some rare occasions it can be appropriate for your child to sleep with you. If your child has been sleeping in your room regularly, work back toward having her sleep in her own bed. Create a ladder of exposures with rewards for sleeping on the floor next to you, then outside of your room, then eventually in her own actual bed.

8. If she makes a habit of getting out of bed, let her know that you'll check on her, rather than her coming to find

you. If she's a repeat come-downstairs-after-she's-gone-to-bed offender, she can request a certain number of times for you to check on her, and the two of you can gradually decrease the number with exposures.

9. Keep bedtime short and sweet. Read one book. Sing one song. Say prayers for a specific, brief period. Prolonged bedtimes just make it harder to separate. End each time with a pleasant exchange. It can also help shorten the time to sit rather than lie on her bed.

10. Create a sleep-friendly environment. Remove clocks from her room, including any phones or tablets. Use low-voltage lighting. Certain essential oils can also enhance a sleep-friendly atmosphere.

Acknowledgments

In this book, I talk a lot about how gratitude and anxiety have an inverse relationship. Any anxiety I have should be completely underwater as a result of the giftedness and kindness and cheering on-ness of this group of people.

Amy Cato and Amanda Young, I wouldn't know where I'm traveling, what I'm saying, or which way was up if it weren't for the wisdom, practicality, and compassion of the two of you. Thank you for always steering me in the right direction.

Jeff Braun, thank you for getting this worry-free party started. God prompted you, and I believe He will use you to change many lives—mine included.

Jana Muntsinger, you are unrivaled in your ability not just to do some mighty good PR but to champion those you care about and work with. I'm honored to be in good company with you and Pamela McClure.

Courtney DeFeo, Jeannie Cunnion, and Elisabeth Hasselbeck, being in the trenches of this kind of work with the three of you keeps me feeling deeply inspired and humbled at the same time.

Katie Plunkett, thank you for the creativity and heart you pour into each drawing, poster, party, and social media splash. You are a wonder—and a gift.

Pace Verner, thank you for being an early reader and constant cheerer-on-er.

Daystar Staff family, it is a privilege to stand with you in this mighty work of offering hope to kids and parents. You're doing a phenomenal job.

David, I wouldn't pick anyone else to be the Donny to my Marie. (They're a brother and sister old-school singing duo, for you young folks.) I love getting to do ministry and life and friendship with you daily.

Melissa, your words are echoed through the pages of this book. Thank you for sharing truth and hope and Jesus with me for so many years—and for not just being my friend but also family. And, of course, neighbor. It's not nearly as fun to write a book without you or David.

Kathleen, Aaron, and Henry, I love being your sidekick, play-mate, roommate, and Big Sis/Aunt Sissy. Even having those titles in your lives makes me feel honored and like I want to rise into them more.

And, finally, to all of the girls and families I get to sit with and listen to and walk alongside . . . you've got this. That old Worry Monster has nothing on you. It is a privilege to be a part of your smart, strong, brave stories.

Notes

Introduction

1. Dr. Tamar Chansky, "Welcome to Worrywisekids," WorryWiseKids.org, The Children's and Adult Center for OCD and Anxiety, accessed April 25, 2019, http://www.worrywisekids.org.

2. Raising Boys and Girls, accessed April 24, 2019, http://www.raisingboysandgirls.com/.

Chapter 1: Defining Worry

1. Jena E. Pincott, "Wicked Thoughts," *Psychology Today*, September 1, 2015, https://www.psychologytoday.com/us/articles/201509/wicked-thoughts.

Chapter 2: Why Her?

1. Dr. Tamar Chansky, "Welcome to Worrywisekids," WorryWiseKids.org, The Children's and Adult Center for OCD and Anxiety, accessed April 25, 2019, http://www.worrywisekids.org.

2. Allison Edwards, *Why Smart Kids Worry: And What Parents Can Do to Help* (Naperville, IL: Sourcebooks, 2013), vi.

3. Edwards, *Why Smart Kids Worry*, vi.

4. Tamar E. Chansky, *Freeing Your Child from Anxiety: Practical Strategies to Overcome Fears, Worries, and Phobias and Be Prepared for Life—from Toddlers to Teens*, rev. and updated ed. (New York: Harmony Books, 2014), 56.

5. Bridget Flynn Walker, *Anxiety Relief for Kids: On-the-Spot Strategies to Help Your Child Overcome Worry, Panic & Avoidance* (Oakland, CA: New Harbinger Publications, Inc., 2017), 8.

6. Chansky, *Freeing Your Child from Anxiety*, 8.

7. William Stixrud and Ned Johnson, *The Self-Driven Child: The Science and Sense of Giving Your Kids More Control over Their Lives* (New York: Viking, 2018), 8.

8. Stixrud and Johnson, *The Self-Driven Child*, 2.

9. Reid Wilson and Lynn Lyons, *Anxious Kids, Anxious Parents: 7 Ways to Stop the Worry Cycle and Raise Courageous and Independent Children* (Deerfield Beach, FL: Health Communications, Inc., 2013), 17.

10. Perri Klass, "How to Help a Child with an Anxiety Disorder," *New York Times*, October 1, 2018, https://www.nytimes.com/2018/10/01/well/family/how-to-help-a-child-with-an-anxiety-disorder.html.

11. "Any Anxiety Disorder," National Institute of Mental Health, updated November 2017, https://www.nimh.nih.gov/health/statistics/any-anxiety-disorder.shtml.

12. Ron Steingard, "Mood Disorders and Teenage Girls," Child Mind Institute, https://childmind.org/article/mood-disorders-and-teenage-girls/.

13. Chansky, *Freeing Your Child from Anxiety*, 28–29.

14. Leonard Sax, *Girls on the Edge* (New York: Basic Books, 2010), 7.

15. Sax, *Girls on the Edge*, 8.

16. Rachel Simmons, "Teenage Girls Are Facing Impossible Expectations," CNN, February 27, 2018, https://www.cnn.com/2018/02/27/opinions/girls-power-expectation-depression-opinion-simmons/index.html.

17. Edwards, *Why Smart Kids Worry*, 116.

18. Edwards, *Why Smart Kids Worry*, 116.

19. "Eating Disorders Facts and Statistics," The Body Image Therapy Center, accessed April 25, 2019, https://thebodyimagecenter.com/education-awareness/eating-disorder-statistics/.

20. "Eating Disorders Facts," https://thebodyimagecenter.com/education-awareness/eating-disorder-statistics/.

21. "Eating Disorders Facts," https://thebodyimagecenter.com/education-awareness/eating-disorder-statistics/.

22. "Eating Disorders Facts," https://thebodyimagecenter.com/education-awareness/eating-disorder-statistics/.

23. "Eating Disorders Facts," https://thebodyimagecenter.com/education-awareness/eating-disorder-statistics/.

24. Heather R. Gallivan, *Teens, Social Media and Body Image* (St. Louis Park, MN: Park Nicollet Melrose Center), accessed April 25, 2019, http://www.macmh.org/wp-content/uploads/2014/05/18_Gallivan_Teens-social-media-body-image-presentation-H-Gallivan-Spring-2014.pdf.

25. Gallivan, *Teens, Social Media and Body Image*, http://www.macmh.org/wp-content/uploads/2014/05/18_Gallivan_Teens-social-media-body-image-present ation-H-Gallivan-Spring-2014.pdf.

26. Gallivan, *Teens, Social Media and Body Image*, http://www.macmh.org/wp-content/uploads/2014/05/18_Gallivan_Teens-social-media-body-image-present ation-H-Gallivan-Spring-2014.pdf.

27. Robin Marantz Henig, "Understanding the Anxious Mind," *New York Times Magazine*, September 29, 2009, https://www.nytimes.com/2009/10/04/magazine/04anxiety-t.html.

28. Chansky, *Freeing Your Child from Anxiety*, 34.

29. "Trauma," American Psychological Association, accessed April 25, 2019, https://www.apa.org/topics/trauma/.

30. Bridget Flynn Walker, *Anxiety Relief for Kids: On-the-Spot Strategies to Help Your Child Overcome Worry, Panic & Avoidance* (Oakland, CA: New Harbinger, 2017), 11.

31. Chansky, *Freeing Your Child from Anxiety*, 34.

32. Wilson and Lyons, *Anxious Kids, Anxious Parents*, 26.

33. Wilson and Lyons, *Anxious Kids, Anxious Parents*, 26.

34. Chansky, *Freeing Your Child from Anxiety*, 32–33.

35. Wilson and Lyons, *Anxious Kids, Anxious Parents*, 35.

36. Carina Wolff, "If You Have These 7 Habits, You Might Have High-Functioning Anxiety," *Bustle*, June 19, 2018, https://www.bustle.com/p/if-you-have-these-7-habits-you-might-have-high-functioning-anxiety-9445027.

37. Stixrud and Johnson, *The Self-Driven Child*, 86.

38. Sissy Goff, David Thomas, and Melissa Trevathan, *Are My Kids on Track?: The 12 Emotional, Social and Spiritual Milestones Your Child Needs to Reach* (Bloomington, MN: Bethany House, 2017), 15.

39. Cathy Creswell, Monika Parkinson, Kerstin Thirlwall, and Lucy Willetts, *Parent-Led CBT for Child Anxiety: Helping Parents Help Their Kids* (New York: The Guilford Press, 2017), 42.

40. Andrea Petersen, "The Right Way for Parents to Help Anxious Children," *Wall Street Journal*, December 8, 2017, https://www.wsj.com/articles/the-right-way-for-parents-to-help-anxious-children-1512755970.

41. Creswell et al., *Parent-Led CBT*, 66–67.

42. Julie Lythcott-Haims, *How to Raise an Adult: Break Free of the Overparenting Trap and Prepare Your Kid for Success* (New York: St. Martin's Griffin, 2015), 89.

43. Creswell et al., *Parent-Led CBT*, 66.

44. Stixrud and Johnson, *The Self-Driven Child*, 89.

45. Lythcott-Haims, *How to Raise an Adult*, 94.

46. Andrea Peterson, "The Right Way for Parents to Help Anxious Children," *Wall Street Journal*, December 8, 2017, https://www.wsj.com/articles/the-right-way-for-parents-to-help-anxious-children-1512755970.

47. Stixrud and Johnson, *The Self-Driven Child*, 83.

Chapter 3: How Will This Help?

1. Perri Klass, "Kids' Suicide-Related Hospital Visits Rise Sharply," *New York Times*, May 16, 2018, https://www.nytimes.com/2018/05/16/well/family/suicide-adolescents-hospital.html.

2. Fyodor Dostoyevsky, *Winter Notes on Summer Impressions*, trans. David Patterson (Evanston, IL: Northwestern University Press, 1997), 49.

3. Lea Winerman, "Suppressing the 'White Bears'," *Monitor on Psychology*, October 2011, https://www.apa.org/monitor/2011/10/unwanted-thoughts.

4. David A. Clark and Aaron T. Beck, *The Anxiety and Worry Workbook: The Cognitive Behavioral Solution* (New York: The Guilford Press, 2012), 41, 51.

5. Bridget Flynn Walker, *Anxiety Relief for Kids: On-the-Spot Strategies to Help Your Child Overcome Worry, Panic & Avoidance* (Oakland, CA: New Harbinger Publications, Inc., 2017), 20.

6. Perri Klass, "How to Help a Child with an Anxiety Disorder," *New York Times*, October 1, 2018, https://www.nytimes.com/2018/10/01/well/family/how-to-help-a-child-with-an-anxiety-disorder.html.

7. Sissy Goff, David Thomas, and Melissa Trevathan, *Are My Kids on Track?: The 12 Emotional, Social and Spiritual Milestones Your Child Needs to Reach* (Bloomington, MN: Bethany House, 2017), 105.

8. *Pooh's Grand Adventure: The Search for Christopher Robin*, 1997, written by Carter Crocker and Karl Geurs, distributed by Walt Disney Home Video, United States.

Chapter 4: Help for Her Body

1. Cathy Creswell, Monika Parkinson, Kerstin Thirlwall, and Lucy Willetts, *Parent-Led CBT for Child Anxiety: Helping Parents Help Their Kids* (New York: The Guilford Press, 2017), 3.

2. Kristen Domonell, "This Is Your Body on Fear," *Right as Rain*, October 25, 2017, https://rightasrain.uwmedicine.org/well/health/your-body-fear-anxiety.

3. Daniel Evans, as paraphrased from Domonell, "This Is Your Body on Fear."

4. David A. Clark and Aaron T. Beck, *The Anxiety and Worry Workbook: The Cognitive Behavioral Solution* (New York: The Guilford Press, 2012), 34.

5. Robert M. Sapolsky, "How to Relieve Stress," *Greater Good*, University of California, Berkeley, March 22, 2012, https://greatergood.berkeley.edu/article/item/how_to_relieve_stress.

6. Daniel J. Siegel and Tina Payne Bryson, *The Yes Brain: How to Cultivate Courage, Curiosity, and Resilience in Your Child* (New York: Bantam Books, 2018), 17.

7. William Stixrud and Ned Johnson, *The Self-Driven Child: The Science and Sense of Giving Your Kids More Control over Their Lives* (New York: Viking, 2018), 23.

8. Reid Wilson and Lynn Lyons, *Anxious Kids, Anxious Parents: 7 Ways to Stop the Worry Cycle and Raise Courageous and Independent Children* (Deerfield Beach, FL: Health Communications, Inc., 2013), 16.

9. Denise B. Lacher, Todd Nichols, Melissa Nichols, and Joanne C. May, *Connecting with Kids through Stories: Using Narratives to Facilitate Attachment in Adopted Children*, 2nd ed. (London: Jessica Kingsley Publishers, 2012), 32.

10. Tamar E. Chansky, *Freeing Your Child from Anxiety: Practical Strategies to Overcome Fears, Worries, and Phobias and Be Prepared for Life—from Toddlers to Teens*, rev. and updated ed. (New York: Harmony Books, 2014), 81.

11. Mayo Clinic Staff, "Mindfulness Exercises," Mayo Clinic, August 17, 2018, https://www.mayoclinic.org/healthy-lifestyle/consumer-health/in-depth/mindfulness-exercises/art-20046356.

12. Alice G. Walton, "Mindfulness Meditation May Help Treat Anxiety Disorders," *Forbes*, January 26, 2017, https://www.forbes.com/sites/alicegwalton/2017/01/26/mindfulness-meditation-may-help-treat-anxiety-disorders/#3d12473b12ad.

13. Dawn Huebner, *What to Do When You Worry Too Much: A Kid's Guide to Overcoming Anxiety* (Washington, D.C.: Magination Press, 2006), 5.

14. David Rock, "Announcing the Healthy Mind Platter," *Psychology Today*, June 2, 2011, https://www.psychologytoday.com/us/blog/your-brain-work/201106/announcing-the-healthy-mind-platter.

15. Rock, "Announcing the Healthy Mind Platter," https://www.psychologytoday.com/us/blog/your-brain-work/201106/announcing-the-healthy-mind-platter.

16. Siegel and Bryson, *The Yes Brain*, 58.

17. Stixrud and Johnson, *The Self-Driven Child*, 19–20.

18. Stixrud and Johnson, *The Self-Driven Child*, 20.

19. Siegel and Bryson, *The Yes Brain*, 62.

20. Gareth Cook, "The Case for the Self-Driven Child," *Scientific American*, February 13, 2018, https://www.scientificamerican.com/article/the-case-for-the-ldquo-self-driven-child-rdquo/.

21. Stixrud and Johnson, *The Self-Driven Child*, 15.

Chapter 5: Help for Her Mind

1. Sun Tzu, *The Art of War* (Greyhound Press, 1910, 2017), 9.

2. Alina Tugend, "Praise Is Fleeting, but Brickbats We Recall," *New York Times*, March 23, 2012, https://www.nytimes.com/2012/03/24/your-money/why-people-remember-negative-events-more-than-positive-ones.html.

3. Allison Edwards, *Why Smart Kids Worry: And What Parents Can Do to Help* (Naperville, IL: Sourcebooks, 2013), 168.

4. Tamar E. Chansky, *Freeing Your Child from Anxiety: Practical Strategies to Overcome Fears, Worries, and Phobias and Be Prepared for Life—from Toddlers to Teens*, rev. and updated ed. (New York: Harmony Books, 2014), 11.

5. Chansky, *Freeing Your Child from Anxiety*, 14.

6. *This Is Us*, season 2, episode 18, "The Wedding," directed by Glenn Ficarra, John Requa, and Ken Olin, written by Dan Fogelman, aired March 13, 2018, on NBC.

7. Dan B. Allender, *The Healing Path: How the Hurts in Your Past Can Lead You to a More Abundant Life* (Colorado Springs: WaterBrook, 1999), 189.

8. Chansky, *Freeing Your Child from Anxiety*, 203.

9. Daniel J. Siegel and Mary Hartzell, *Parenting from the Inside Out: How a Deeper Self-Understanding Can Help You Raise Children Who Thrive* (New York: Tarcher Publishing, 2003), 58.

Chapter 6: Help for Her Heart

1. Dawn Huebner, *Outsmarting Worry: An Older Kid's Guide to Managing Anxiety* (London: Jessica Kingsley Publishers, 2018), 10.

2. Bridget Flynn Walker, *Anxiety Relief for Kids: On-the-Spot Strategies to Help Your Child Overcome Worry, Panic & Avoidance* (Oakland, CA: New Harbinger Publications, Inc., 2017), 142.

3. David A. Clark and Aaron T. Beck, *The Anxiety and Worry Workbook: The Cognitive Behavioral Solution* (New York: The Guilford Press, 2012), 83.

4. Walker, *Anxiety Relief for Kids*, 58.

5. Daniel J. Siegel and Tina Payne Bryson, *The Yes Brain: How to Cultivate Courage, Curiosity, and Resilience in Your Child* (New York: Bantam Books, 2018), 85.

6. Walker, *Anxiety Relief for Kids*, 56.

7. William Stixrud and Ned Johnson, *The Self-Driven Child: The Science and Sense of Giving Your Kids More Control over Their Lives* (New York: Viking, 2018), 32.

8. Walker, *Anxiety Relief for Kids*, 20.

9. "What Is Exposure Therapy?," American Psychological Association, accessed April 25, 2019, https://www.apa.org/ptsd-guideline/patients-and-families/exposure -therapy.

10. Elizabeth DuPont Spencer, Robert L. DuPont, and Caroline M. DuPont, *The Anxiety Cure for Kids: A Guide for Parents* (New York: John Wiley & Sons, Inc., 2014), 3.

11. Cathy Creswell, Monika Parkinson, Kerstin Thirlwall, and Lucy Willetts, *Parent-Led CBT for Child Anxiety: Helping Parents Help Their Kids* (New York: The Guilford Press, 2017), 120.

12. Wilson and Lyons, *Anxious Kids, Anxious Parents*, 102.

13. Wilson and Lyons, *Anxious Kids, Anxious Parents*, 120.

14. Wilson and Lyons, *Anxious Kids, Anxious Parents*, 91.

Chapter 7: Trouble

1. Daniel J. Siegel and Tina Payne Bryson, *The Yes Brain: How to Cultivate Courage, Curiosity, and Resilience in Your Child* (New York: Bantam, 2018), 120.

2. Siegel and Bryson, *The Yes Brain*, 82.

3. Associated Press, "Va. Teen Club Volleyball Player Suing after Getting Benched," *Fox 5*, April 1, 2015, http://www.fox5dc.com/news/va-teen-club-volleyball-player -suing-after-getting-benched.

4. Laura Santhanam, "Suicide Rate Rising Fastest among Women, CDC Says," PBS.org, June 14, 2018, https://www.pbs.org/newshour/health/suicide-rate-rising -fastest-among-women-cdc-says.

5. Jon Blum, "Global Depression and Anxiety," *Medium*, March 4, 2017, https:// medium.com/@blumfest/global-depression-and-anxiety-148afd856432, reporting on estimates from the World Health Organization, *Depression and Other Common Mental Disorders: Global Health Estimates* (Geneva: World Health Organization, 2017), https://apps.who.int/iris/bitstream/handle/10665/254610/WHO-MSD-MER -2017.2-eng.pdf;jsessionid=3C066D350D7C8E8630F9F3DF6844E976.

6. David A. Clark and Aaron T. Beck, *The Anxiety and Worry Workbook: The Cognitive Behavioral Solution* (New York: The Guilford Press, 2012), 237.

Chapter 8: Take Heart

1. Shakespeare, *A Midsummer Night's Dream*, ed. Trevor R. Griffiths (Cambridge: Cambridge University Press, 1996), 3.2.325. References are to act, scene, and line.

2. *The Chronicles of Narnia: Prince Caspian*, directed by Andrew Adamson (Burbank, CA: Walt Disney Home Entertainment, 2008), DVD.

3. HELPS Word-studies, https://biblehub.com/greek/2293.htm.

4. Henri Nouwen, *Making All Things New: An Invitation to the Spiritual Life* (New York: HarperCollins, 1981), 37.

5. Nouwen, *Making All Things New*, 82–83.

6. Pierre Teilhard de Chardin, SJ, "Patient Trust," in Michael Harter, SJ, ed., *Hearts on Fire: Praying with Jesuits* (Chicago: Loyola Press, 2005), 102.

7. Biblehub.com

8. William Stixrud and Ned Johnson, *The Self-Driven Child: The Science and Sense of Giving Your Kids More Control over Their Lives* (New York: Viking, 2018), 95–103.

9. Stixrud and Johnson, *The Self-Driven Child*, 95–103.

10. The Serenity Prayer, attributed to Reinhold Neibuhr, quoted in "Serenity Prayer—Applying 3 Truths from the Bible," Crosswalk.com, January 12, 2017, http s://www.crosswalk.com/faith/prayer/serenity-prayer-applying-3-truths-from-the -bible.html.

11. David A. Clark and Aaron T. Beck, *The Anxiety and Worry Workbook: The Cognitive Behavioral Solution* (New York: The Guilford Press, 2012), 83.

12. Frederick Buechner, *Whistling in the Dark: A Doubter's Dictionary* (San Francisco: HarperSanFrancisco, 1988, 1993), 12.

13. David G. Benner, *Sacred Companions: The Gift of Spiritual Friendship & Direction* (Downers Grove, IL: InterVarsity Press, 2002), 94.

14. Amy Morin, "7 Scientifically Proven Benefits of Gratitude That Will Motivate You to Give Thanks Year-Round," *Forbes*, November 23, 2014, https://www .forbes.com/sites/amymorin/2014/11/23/7-scientifically-proven-benefits-of-gratit ude-that-will-motivate-you-to-give-thanks-year-round/.

15. Tamar E. Chansky, *Freeing Your Child from Anxiety: Practical Strategies to Overcome Fears, Worries, and Phobias and Be Prepared for Life—from Toddlers to Teens*, rev. and updated ed. (New York: Harmony Books, 2014), 165.

Chapter 9: Overcomer

1. Anne Lamott, Facebook, November 7, 2013, https://www.facebook.com/Anne Lamott/photos/a.120197964776522/400007300128919/?type=1&theater.

2. David A. Clark and Aaron T. Beck, *The Anxiety and Worry Workbook: The Cognitive Behavioral Solution* (New York: The Guilford Press, 2012), 247.

Appendix 1: Types of Anxiety

1. Tamar E. Chansky, *Freeing Your Child from Anxiety: Practical Strategies to Overcome Fears, Worries, and Phobias and Be Prepared for Life—from Toddlers to Teens*, rev. and updated ed. (New York: Harmony Books, 2014), 29.

2. Obsessive Compulsive Foundation of Metropolitan Chicago, *How to Help Your Child*, 3, https://adaa.org/sites/default/files/How-to-Help-Your-Child-A -Parents-Guide-to-OCD.pdf.

3. Chansky, *Freeing Your Child from Anxiety*, 334.

4. Chansky, *Freeing Your Child from Anxiety*, 255.

5. Chansky, *Freeing Your Child from Anxiety*, 344.

6. Chansky, *Freeing Your Child from Anxiety*, 344.

7. "Diagnosing Tic Disorders," Centers for Disease Control and Prevention, accessed April 24, 2019, https://www.cdc.gov/ncbddd/tourette/diagnosis.html.

Appendix 2: Beating the Bedtime Blues

1. Tamar E. Chansky, *Freeing Your Child from Anxiety: Practical Strategies to Overcome Fears, Worries, and Phobias and Be Prepared for Life—from Toddlers to Teens*, rev. and updated ed. (New York: Harmony Books, 2014), 379.

Sissy Goff, M.Ed., LPC-MHSP, spends most of her days counseling girls and their families, with the help of her assistant/pet therapist, Lucy the Havanese. Since 1993, Sissy has worked as the director of child and adolescent counseling at Daystar Counseling Ministries. She speaks to parents and children's ministers across the country and is a frequent guest on media outlets, including *Focus on the Family*, *FamilyLife Today*, and *The 700 Club*. She lives in Nashville.

More from Sissy Goff

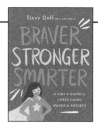

This teen-friendly guide—for girls ages 13 to 18—from counselor Sissy Goff will help your daughter understand anxiety's roots and why her brain is often working against her when she worries. Filled with stories and self-discovery exercises, she will find more of her voice and her confidence, discovering the brave girl God made her to be.

Brave

This illustrated guide for girls ages 6 to 11 will help your daughter see how brave, strong, and smart God made her. Through easy-to-read stories and writing and drawing prompts, she will learn practical ways to fight back when worries come up and will feel empowered knowing she is deeply loved by a God who is bigger than her fears.

Braver, Stronger, Smarter

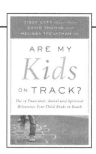

From birth our children's physical and intellectual development is carefully charted. But how do we know their hearts are on track? Filled with wisdom, research, and practical advice, this book shows how you can help your child reach 12 key emotional, social, and spiritual benchmarks that will shape the type of spouse, parent, and friend they will become.

Are My Kids on Track?

◊ BETHANY HOUSE

Stay up to date on your favorite books and authors with our free e-newsletters. Sign up today at bethanyhouse.com.

 facebook.com/BHPnonfiction

 @bethany_house

 @bethany_house_nonfiction